tag rugby

796
⎯⎯
334

Y ΠF

Jane Liddiard

tag | rugby

everything you need to play and coach

A & C Black • London

Published in 2006 by A & C Black Publishers Ltd
38 Soho Square, London W1D 3HB
www.acblack.com

Copyright © 2006 Jane Liddiard

ISBN-10: 0 7136 7740 6
ISBN-13: 978 0 7136 7740 9

A CIP record for this book is available from the British Library.

Note: While every effort has been made to ensure that the content of this book is as technically accurate and as sound as possible, neither the author nor the publisher can accept responsibility for any injury or loss sustained as a result of the use of this material.

A & C Black uses paper produced with elemental chlorine-free pulp, harvested from managed sustainable forests.

Acknowledgements
Cover photographs © ActionPlus Images (top) and iStockphoto (bottom)
Photograph on p107/8 © Russell Clarke, Prophoto – Queens Park Studio, Bournemouth, UK, reproduced by kind permission
Other textual photographs © The Bridge
Illustrations by Dave Saunders
Cover and inside design by James Wakelin

Printed and bound in Great Britain by MPG Books Ltd, Bodmin.

For my nephew
Oliver Burton

contents

acknowledgements

Special thanks to my editors Charlotte Croft and Claire Dunn for their help, encouragement and professional advice; to Nick Bunting at the RFU for giving his time and information; to Will Greenwood MBE at Harlequins RFC for his foreword; to Richard Varney and Nick Melton at Harlequins RFC; and to my brother Jon Burton at Salisbury RFC, and Harlequins supporters the Mallet family and tag rugby coach Martin Wilson for their valuable help and co-operation.

Personal thanks go to my husband John for his patience and unflagging support; to my son Alastair for his expert advice and my son James for his interest and support; to my very good friends and fellow writers Lucy Daniel Raby and Colleen Curran and to my special friend Pat Barden for their faith in me and support for my writing over the years.

Crown copyright material for the National Curriculum is reproduced with the permission of the Controller of HMSO and the Queen's Printer for Scotland.

foreword

Since England won the World Cup in 2003, beating Australia 20–17, the exciting game of rugby football has become increasingly popular. For someone like me, who played in that final, tense and triumphant match in Sydney, it is particularly gratifying to see that community rugby has benefited hugely from this success.

Community rugby begins with tag rugby, the non-contact version of the game, which can safely be played by boys and girls together as young as five years old. Players then progress to junior and senior rugby and, for the really talented players, there is the chance of a place at a rugby Academy. The stars of the future depend on this enthusiasm for the game at club and school level and tag rugby is vital for instilling a love of playing the game for all, as well as for bringing on gifted players.

Tag rugby coaches and teachers – both absolute beginners and those with know-ledge of how to play the game – will find this book invaluable. Using clear, simple language, diagrams, exercises and games as well as lesson plans, all based on the RFU's own rules and instructions, dedicated rugby enthusiast and former teacher Jane Liddiard has produced an excellent book that will guide you through tag rugby step by step. There are also chapters on refereeing, guidelines for working with children and health and safety, as well as essential information for starting up a club or school team, entering festivals and competitions, playing at local and professional grounds on match days and finding extra funds, and you'll also find information about my own club Harlequins.

Using this book will improve your coaching and playing skills and, above all, ensure that tag rugby is immensely enjoyed by both players and spectators alike.

Will Greenwood MBE
England and British Lions International
Harlequins Rugby Football Club

1

1 what is tag rugby?

Tag rugby is a safe, non-contact, easy-to-play evasion game. It is suitable for both adults and children, but this book deals with tag rugby for Under-10s in primary schools and community clubs. It is aimed at teachers (National Curriculum Key Stages 1 and 2), coaches and referees, but is also a good read for anyone interested in playing or watching tag rugby.

Tag rugby has been specifically developed by the Rugby Football Union (RFU) for very young children. In the past, young children and their parents have been put off by injuries caused by scrums, mauls and lineouts; such physical activities are now seen as dangerous and inappropriate for young, growing bodies, so a primary school/local community version of mini rugby has been specially developed. The enthusiasm of young children will more than make up for their lack of stature, and the game is particularly good for all-round fitness, running and handling skills, fostering team spirit and becoming a good sport.

So what's different from the normal game?

In the senior game the emphasis is on physical strength as well as skill. If you've ever watched a scrum down, you can't help but gasp when the referee orders 'Engage!' and the two opposing sides hurl themselves forwards to lock neck and shoulders in the front rows. The sheer force of this bone-crunching action always makes me grateful that I'm not in that front row myself! The physicality of rucks and mauls can often result in injury – mostly minor in the form of bruising and cuts, but serious injuries do also occur. It's part of the game but, however exciting these aspects of the game appear to be, they are only suitable for mature adults who spend a great deal of their time training to develop their physique to withstand such pressure.

Young children, whose bones are immature and easily broken, cannot risk injury in this way. Therefore, any part of senior rugby that is considered to be a risk in this area has been taken out of the game for minis. Tag rugby has been specially developed by the RFU to start very young players off in schools and in the community. It avoids physical contact altogether so that young children are at a minimal risk of injury and do not associate the game of rugby with being hurt.

They can enjoy the excitement of the game in relative safety and become part of England's fantastic rugby tradition, getting a taste and enthusiasm for the game that will hopefully carry over into junior and then senior rugby. This is important because mini and junior rugby will bring youngsters with a particular talent through to the academies and, hopefully, to a professional career. Even if young players don't become the talented few, they can go on to play rugby at community club level or become passionate supporters, which is just as vital for the success of professional rugby at regional, national and international levels. For example, it was very inspiring to see junior rugby players madly practising their goal kicks the day after Jonny Wilkinson's drop goal secured victory for England in the 2003 World Cup: they were all dreaming of being future World Cup winners.

How is it played?

In a nutshell, tag rugby is played between two teams of equal number (from four to seven players a side). The objective is to score a try by running with the ball from your own half of the pitch into the opposition's half and crossing over the opposition's goal line, carrying the ball in both hands, without being stopped by having your tag taken (the equivalent of being tackled). Tries are scored by grounding the ball with downward pressure, with both hands on the ball and both feet on the ground, or simply by running across the goal line with the ball in both hands – it's as simple as that. The playing surface is usually the decider. If it's hard, such as concrete or tarmac, or there is a fence or wall as a boundary, it's safer not to bend over to ground the ball. In this case, crossing the line is sufficient for a try to be scored. However, whatever the surface being played on, even if it is fairly soft, for safety reasons players must not dive over the line as they do in senior rugby. *They must stay on their feet and bend down to score a try.*

The rugby ball must always be passed behind or laterally (straight across) to another player when the ball carrier is running towards the opponent's goal line. It may not be passed to a player who is in front of the ball carrier, known as a 'forward pass'.

Each player wears two tags on either side of his or her waist on a belt, as shown below. The tags are attached to the belt by Velcro strips and are easy to grab. If a player's tag is detached by an opposing player, the tagger must shout 'Tag!' and hold up the tag as evidence. The referee will shout 'Tag pass!' and the tagged player must then stop running with the ball. If no infringement has taken place, the game will be restarted from where the tagging took place by the player who was tagged. That player must stand still and pass the ball within three seconds. If, however, an infringement has been committed by the tagged player's team, the ball is passed to the defending side and the game is restarted with a free pass from where the offence took place.

Players wearing tags and tag belt

The tags are made of strips of strong material, natural or synthetic, which may be in a team's colours or carry the logo of a sponsor. Each team should have a different coloured tag from their opponents for easy identification.

There is no physical contact of any kind in tag rugby. Physical contact is defined as grabbing hold of an opponent, bringing them down, pulling at a shirt or fending off with an arm or hand. The ball carrier can only be legitimately stopped by his or her tag being taken by an opponent.

The full rules are in Chapter 2, but the following will give you an overview of the game.

How many players?

Teams can be made up of as few as four players, but for competitive matches there should be no fewer than five and no more than seven a side. There must be the same number of players on each side. Once players get used to the rules, it should be possible for teams not playing in a competition to organise themselves without a teacher or club trainer refereeing all the time.

Field of play

Tag rugby is played on a rectangular pitch with a try lines at each end. No goal posts are needed as there are no kicks at all, not even at goal. Teams playing on a full-size rugby or soccer pitch can play across the width of the pitch, which means that several games can be played on one pitch.

Teams can be made up of as few as four players up to a maximum of seven. The dimensions of a seven-a-side pitch are 55–60 m × 30–35 m; if there are only four or five players on each team, the pitch can be reduced to 30–35 m × 15–20 m.

There is a centre line and two 7 m lines, measured either side of the centre line. The corners can be marked by cones for ordinary play, but in competitions or festivals the pitch will need to be marked out correctly with white lines, as shown in Fig. 1.1.

Figure 1.1 | Tag rugby pitch dimensions

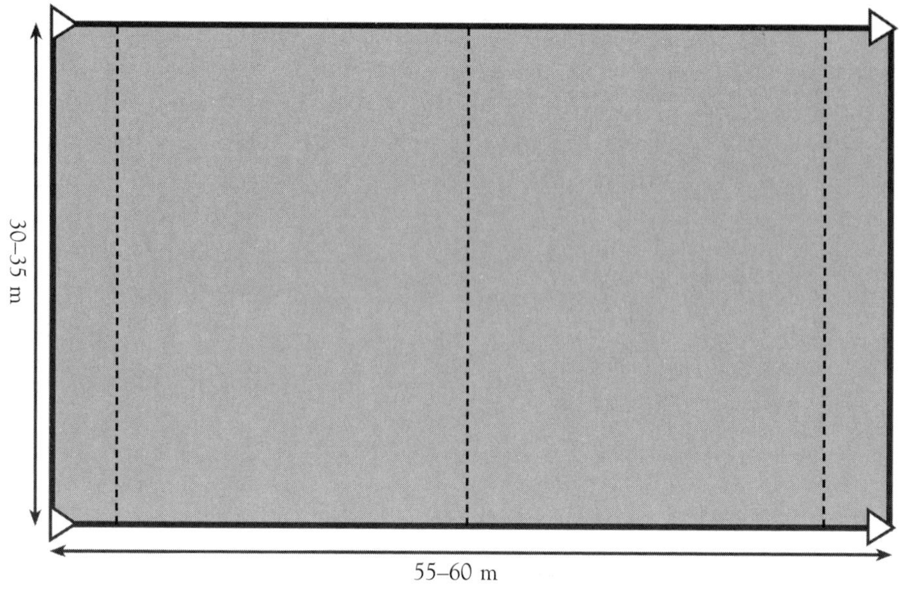

30–35 m

55–60 m

Problems?

Headteachers and tag rugby coaches I have spoken to say that one of the biggest problems when playing other schools or clubs is the lack of common rules. In particular, the size of the pitch may not be the same, or the number of players in the team, tackling rules and so on may be different. If your players are used to playing on one size of pitch, it can be disconcerting for them to find themselves on a larger or smaller pitch. A simple answer to this is to agree the pitch size beforehand with the school or club you will be playing. You can then mark out your pitch to match their dimensions so that your teams can practise and prepare on the same size pitch, so your players won't be at a disadvantage. The same applies to team size. Agree the numbers with your opponents and practise with the same size teams before you arrive at the school or club.

What to wear

Children should wear the following:

- sports shirts and shorts, or track suits, with tops tucked in;

- sports shoes, or rugby boots if children have them and they are playing on grass. If boots are worn, the teacher, coach or referee should check that they are approved by the IRB (world governing and law-making body for rugby union). The right studs are very important and should bear the kite mark;

- tag belts and tags: the belts are worn around the waist with the tags hanging down on either side of the hips. No parts of the tag belt should flap when the belt has been secured around the waist – the ends should be tucked firmly out of the way. This is important in preventing injury to the players;

- mouth guards: the RFU strongly recommends that mouth guards are worn for protection against collision. Preferably, these should be made from an impression of the player's teeth by a dentist or dental technician. However, these can be very expensive and less expensive ones from do-it-yourself kits can be bought.

Matching strip

It's not necessary for clothing to match for school lessons or at local community clubs, but it is helpful if the team tags match. In competitions each team wears its own colours.

Equipment

- One rugby ball per game (see below)
- Two velcro tags attached to a belt for each player.
- Cones or similar to mark out the corners and centre line.

The rugby ball

A rugby ball is egg-shaped. One of the best aspects of the game of rugby at any level is the shape of the ball, as it makes play so unpredictable.

Egg-shaped!

Weird shape or what? The ball has four panels stitched together. In the past these were made of leather, making the ball quite heavy and prone to getting very wet. Leather balls were produced right up to the 1980s, but by then synthetic materials began to be used. Today a rugby ball is made of hi-spec materials that don't get the ball so wet and help to keep its shape. A senior rugby ball is 280–300 mm in length and weighs around 410–440 g, although smaller balls are generally used for junior teams and size 3 balls are used for minis.

Duration of play

A match is made up of two halves, each of 10 minutes duration, with a two-minute interval at half time. It is very important to be aware that tag rugby should be fun, not overly competitive.

Starting play

Play begins when the two teams have lined up across the width of the pitch, in their own halves on either side of the centre line. The teams should face towards each other. The team that won the toss begins with a free pass when the referee blows his or her whistle.

Who can play?

Everybody! Adults and children of all ages, and female and male in mixed teams, can all play. However, this book is aimed at boys and girls aged from 5 to 10 playing tag rugby together in their year groups in schools, or in a close mix of ages in clubs.

Tag rugby will develop a varying range of skills and fitness levels, but does not depend exclusively upon individuals who excel at ball skills such as kicking. The emphasis is on agile running and ball handling, but it's not boring. It can be fast and exciting and will improve agility and team spirit.

Children with learning difficulties and disabled children

If you have children with learning difficulties in your school or club, there is no reason why they shouldn't play tag rugby. In fact, the Disability Discrimination Acts of 1995 and 2005 (DDA 1995 and DDA 2005) make it illegal to exclude children with a disability from such activities. The DDAs aren't there to make your life more difficult, but to make the lives of disabled children easier and more inclusive.

At tag rugby level most children should be able to grasp the simple concepts of the game and achieve the skills necessary to be part of a team.

Problems?

If there are problems, particularly with a physically disabled child, you will need to consult with the parents or carers about the level of involvement that they think is suitable for their child. The child should also have a say in what they feel they can do, then all parties concerned can decide whether it is possible for that child to play. Initially, a child should be encouraged to play normally with the team; you will then be in a better position to assess whether they need further help.

Tasks for non-players

There are lots of tasks that non-players can perform, such as keeping the score, handing out and collecting tags, being near the try line to ensure that tries are scored correctly or giving calls. They can also help the teacher/coach to give advice at half-time and the end of the game. Inclusion in whatever capacity is the key.

Children who are struggling

If you notice that any child, whether they are disabled or not, is really struggling and becoming disheartened, discuss this with the child to see if you can pinpoint what the problem is. It may be a lack of confidence, but there may be other, more serious reasons not connected with rugby. You will find further information about this in Chapter 8.

If it's simply a matter of lacking in confidence or skill, ask if she or he would like to continue running with the ball until two tags have been removed instead of one. The tagger only shouts 'Tag!' when the second tag has been taken, which will give the player extra time and space to make their run. If you decide that this course of action should be taken for a particular child, talk to the others in the team and get them to understand that it isn't favouritism or giving an unfair advantage. Explain how the problem can be solved with their help and co-operation, but do not discuss confidential personal affairs about that child with any other players.

Obviously, it will be difficult to change the rules at competition level; however, as with the Paralympics, it is possible to arrange for disabled teams to play and compete on their own level.

Wheelchairs or other mobility restrictions

If there is a child who uses a wheelchair, or is unable to take part for some other medical reason, you can still involve them in the game. Ask him or her to be a touch judge on the goal line to make sure that the ball is grounded properly. You can also get them to keep a record of the score in a notebook. If you are refereeing you will, of course, need to keep a record of the score yourself, but you can compare notes with your touch judge during the match and at half and full time. See Chapter 7 for more information on this.

Involve them

Above all, don't be frightened of disabled children involving themselves in sport. My elder son has epilepsy and played rugby at senior level as a flanker and on the wing. He wore headgear to protect himself, but this didn't always prevent a seizure. When he did have a seizure during a match, he notified the nearest players and took himself to the sideline for safety. His team-mates knew about his condition and were able to ensure that he didn't harm himself. Needless to say, he didn't continue to play the rest of that match, but he was back in the game as soon as possible after his recovery!

Disabled athletes

Sir Steve Redgrave, the Olympic gold medal rower, has diabetes; Tom Smith, Scotland and Lions prop forward has epilepsy; Tanni Grey-Thompson won 13 medals, 9 of them gold, in her wheelchair at the 2004 Paralympics.

2

2 | **the rules**

This chapter lists the rules as set out by the RFU.

Tries and scoring

The object of tag rugby is to score more tries than the other team. Scoring tries is the only method of scoring in tag rugby: there are no goalposts and no kicking of any kind.

How many points is a try worth?

In tag rugby for U10s it is recommended that a try is worth one point. In games for older children or adults tries may be worth five points, but in mini rugby totalling up five points each time a try is scored may amass many points for one side and dishearten the other. For example, if five tries are scored by one side and only one by the other, it looks better for the result to be 5–1 than 25–5.

How are tries scored?

Tries are scored by placing the ball on the ground behind the opponents' goal line using downward pressure, with the ball in both hands and the player on his or her feet. After a try has been scored the game is restarted from the centre of the pitch with a free pass by the team that did not score the try (see below for more information on free passes).

Correct grounding of the ball over the try line

Rules for scoring tries

When a player crosses the opponents' goal line he or she must:

- be carrying the ball in both hands
- place it on the ground with both hands: note that grounding the ball is not necessary on hard surfaces or playing areas that may have potential hazards
- stay on his/her feet – no diving
- have both tags intact, or if tagged have taken only one stride across the goal line.

Any infringement of these four rules will result in a free pass being given to the opposing team.

Hard surfaces

If the game is being played on a hard surface such as concrete or tarmac, or there is very restricted space beyond the goal line due to a boundary such as a wall or fencing, this is a potential hazard and could cause injury. In this case the ball does not have to be grounded. Instead, players may score a try simply by crossing the goal line with the ball held in both hands, which allows them to stay on their feet, keep their head up and avoid running into any obstacles.

Allowed

If a player is tagged but grounds the ball legally over the goal line within one stride, a try is awarded.

Not allowed

- Dropping the ball over the goal line: this will result in no try and is treated as a knock-on (see page 20 for more information on knock-ons); a free pass is awarded to the other team.
- If a player is tagged but grounds the ball over the goal line by taking more than one stride.
- Grounding the ball with one hand: players must use both hands to hold the ball at all times.
- Diving over the goal line: this looks great in senior rugby but could result in injury for very young players, which is why it is not allowed in tag rugby.
- A ball-carrying player, who is trying to score a goal, fending or handing off an opponent who is attempting a tag. No physical contact is permitted even when

trying to avoid being tagged. The only way a player can avoid being tagged is by running faster than their opponent, or dodging out of the way without barging into anyone else.

Diving onto the ground to score a try is not allowed

All of these offences result in a free pass being given to the opposing team. Most free passes are taken from where the infringement occurred, but for goal line infringements or infringements within 7 m of the goal line, the free pass is taken 7 m from the goal line. This is so the team awarded the free pass is not pinned back on their goal line to restart the game.

After a try is scored

After a try has been scored, the game is restarted with a free pass from the centre of the pitch by the non-scoring side. The player may not run with the ball at the restart, but must pass it to another player, not more than 2 m away, by throwing it through the air backwards before moving. Handing the ball to another player is not allowed.

Ball play

Passing

Passing forwards to a player who is in front of the ball carrier and moving in the direction of the opponent's goal line is not allowed.

Allowed

Backward and lateral passing (level passing sideways) are permitted.

Not allowed

- A forward pass, which is passing the ball to a player who is ahead of the ball carrier.

- Handing the ball to another player: the ball must be thrown.

- Knocking or grabbing the ball out of the hands of the ball carrier.

- Knocking on: this means that the player either throws, drops, or knocks the ball forward.

- Being offside: this can only occur at the restart immediately after a tag. All players from the tagger's team must retreat back towards their goal line so as not to interfere with the restart pass.

All of these infringements result in a free pass being awarded to the opposing team.

Ball being passed backwards – allowed

Ball being passed laterally – allowed

Ball being passed forwards – not allowed

Offside

Free passes

Free passes are taken by standing still and throwing the ball to another player not more than 2 m away. The pass must not be thrown until the referee gives the signal that everyone is ready by shouting 'Play!'

There are four reasons for a free pass:

- To start the game or match at the beginning of each half.

- To restart the game or match after a try has been scored.

- If the ball has gone into touch at the side of the pitch (that is, off the pitch over one of the side lines).

- When an infringement has occurred.

How to take a free pass

The ball carrier must throw the ball to a player no more than 2 m away. The receiver of the pass must start running from within 2 m of the player taking the free pass. The opposing team's players must be 7 m back from the mark where the free pass is being taken. They cannot start moving forwards until the ball leaves the hands of the player taking the free pass.

Not allowed

■ The player taking the free pass may not run with the ball: the ball must be passed to another player with a backward throw before he or she moves.

■ Handing the ball to another player.

■ The receiver not being within 2 m of the player taking the free pass.

■ The opposing team moving forwards before the free pass has been taken.

Removing the tag (tagging)

Removing a tag is the equivalent of a tackle in senior rugby. As discussed, the players wear two tags on either side of the waist, so one or the other tag may be removed by an opposing player holding on to it and pulling. The Velcro strips allow the tag to be removed easily and without excessive force. When a tag has been removed, the tagger must hold up the tag and shout 'Tag!' The referee then responds with 'Tag pass', which means that all players must stop running and the tagged player must quickly take the free pass.

After a tag has been removed, the tagger must hold up the tag and shout 'Tag!'

After a tag is removed – ball carrier

The ball carrier whose tag has been removed must:

- attempt to stop as soon as possible. The RFU recommends that this should be within three strides if possible, but the ball can be passed as the ball carrier is stopping;

- pass the ball within three seconds of being tagged. This includes stopping time;

- retrieve his or her tag as soon as the ball has been passed;

- after being tagged, take only one stride to step over the goal line if going for a try.

Not allowed

- Resuming the game without the tag being returned and reaffixed.

- Snatching the tag back from the tagger.

After a tag is removed – tagger

The tagger must:

- move back towards his or her goal line if within a metre of the tagged player to allow space for the free pass to be taken;

- hand the tag back to the player once the ball has been passed or hand it to the coach or referee, who will hand it back.

Not allowed

- Neither the tagger nor the tagged player may carry on playing and influencing the game until the tag has been handed back and reaffixed.

- The tagger may not throw the tag down and carry on playing.

Infringements

Any infringement should result in a free pass being awarded to the opposing team from the place where the infringement occurred. All of these infringements have been mentioned above, but are included together in this one section to make it easier to identify them.

A) No forward passing

Forward passing occurs when the player receiving the ball is ahead of the player throwing the ball. 'Forward' is defined as 'moving in the direction of the opponent's goal line'.

B) Knock-on

A knock-on occurs when a player does not retain possession in both hands and the ball falls to the ground. It is not always necessary, however, to blow the whistle for this offence if advantage can be played. The non-offending team may be able to pick up the ball and run with it, thereby gaining tactical or territorial advantage.

C) Offside

A player can only be offside immediately after a player has been tagged. Offside occurs if he or she is not behind the ball and is interfering with play. Once a tag has been made, all players from the opposing team must retreat towards their own goal line behind the ball. The non-ball-carrying team should not be penalised, however, if all their players haven't had time to retreat, provided that they are not interfering with play. 'Interfering with play' is when an offside player intercepts or slows down a pass from the tagged player to someone in his or her team. If this occurs, a free pass should be awarded to the tagged player.

However, a player *can* run from an onside position to intercept the ball. In this case there is no infringement and play continues with the team who made the turnover retaining the ball.

D) No dropping or diving onto the ground

In tag rugby players must stay on their feet in order to play the game. Safety and enjoyment and not getting hurt are the keys to successful play. Therefore, there is no:

■ dropping to the ground with the ball in your hands

■ diving on top of a loose ball on the ground

■ diving over the goal line to score a try.

It does not make any difference if any of these infringements are accidental through slipping or overbalancing. A free pass will still be awarded to the opposing team if they happen. If the ball goes to ground through a missed pass, a player from either team may pick up the ball provided he or she stays on their feet.

The only occasion when the ball cannot be picked up from the ground to resume the game is when it goes out of play by going into touch. This will result in a free pass for the team that was not carrying the ball at the time of the infringement.

E) No kicking the ball

No kicking of any kind is allowed in tag rugby.

F) No physical contact

Such infringements occur when a player:

- hands off another player by pushing out a hand towards that player's face or body. Both hands should be on the ball and no handing off is allowed;

- fends off a player by pushing his or her hand out of the way when an attempted tag is taking place. Both hands should be on the ball and no fending off is allowed;

- barges or accidentally runs into another player;

- grabs the clothing of another player;

- tries to hold onto another player in any way;

- pushes another player away;

- brings another player down to the ground.

G) Out of play

The ball goes out of play when the ball carrier steps on or runs over the boundary lines of the pitch, or if the ball itself lands on the line or goes outside the boundaries of the pitch. A free pass is taken inside the playing area from the point where the ball went out of play. However, note that if the ball goes out of play over the goal line, the free pass is taken 7 m from the goal line.

Know these rules

It is important that you and the players know these rules so that you can all abide by them and no one is playing to a different set. However, in the interests of a flowing game the referee should not blow up for every little infringement. Tag rugby is fast and skilful and it's impossible to spot everything that's going on. Also, infringements that don't interfere with play and that are not serious are probably best ignored so that the game can flow. Play advantage wherever possible. This will also ensure that the players don't get disheartened by being constantly penalised and don't lose their concentration.

The rules in a nutshell

1. Field of play to be within RFU's set limits.

2. Equal number of players on each team.

3. Try (scored over goal line) is worth 1 point.

4. Player with the ball must pass behind or laterally.

5. Removing a tag is the equivalent of a tackle.

6. A tag results in a free pass by tagged player within 3 seconds.

7. The tagged player must then retrieve and attach their tag.

8. The tagger must retreat from where the free pass is taken and then hand back the tag.

9. Free passes are awarded for infringements.

10. Infringements include forward passing, knock-on, offside, diving on the ground, kicking, physical contact, ball out of play. All result in a free pass.

11. Restarts after a try are taken with a free pass from the centre line by the non-scoring team.

3

3 | coaching

Before you begin

Take a look at Chapter 8: Guidelines for working with children. This is essential reading or revision before you undertake any kind of work with children in the world of rugby. Even if you think you know everything, it is advisable to check again and remind yourself. The safety and well-being of the children in your care is the most important aspect of your coaching and training. You may not be a bully or abuser yourself, nor running a club badly, but others may be and it is your duty to look out for this and for any other problems with the children in your care. If you suspect something is amiss, make a record of your concerns and then contact the appropriate authority to report it. All the details and information you need for this are contained in Chapter 8.

However, don't be put off by all this. It's all common sense really, but today we are more aware of how children can be maltreated and the children themselves are, quite rightly, aware of their rights and more protected by law than they were in the past. Knowing the guidelines and understanding where to draw the line will also protect you from any mischievous or malicious action against you.

Do the right thing

Any sport can have coaches who are bullies or child abusers somewhere in its ranks, so rugby must not become complacent and think that it could never happen in our sport. Be vigilant. If you suspect something is wrong, take action. It's better to do something for the right intentions and be mistaken than to do nothing at all.

Safety first

If you are coaching children, you should not only have a well-equipped first-aid kit handy, but should also have good first-aid knowledge, preferably having attended a course run by the St John Ambulance, your local council or a similar organisation. Don't be fooled into thinking 'it's only a few kids running around, so where's the harm in that?' The fact is that an injury can happen at any time and can often be caused by something that may appear perfectly innocuous. A player can roll over on an ankle, slip or fall, and while this may not necessarily lead to an injury, it could do – so be prepared.

There may also be some children in the group with pre-existing medical conditions. You will therefore need to know what to do if a player has an epileptic seizure or goes into anaphylactic shock. Encourage the children and their parents or carers to let you know of any potential medical problems. This will enable you to plan your coaching or teaching sessions more effectively and safely.

Already had some experience?

Make sure you really know the basic rules of tag rugby as set out in Chapter 2 and get someone to test you, or test yourself.

New to all this?

Where do you start out as a coach? If you're a PE teacher you will have the advantage of ready-made facilities and captive players so you won't need to look for venues and basic equipment. However, all coaches and teachers will need to acquire coaching skills, learn the RFU's Rules of Tag Rugby and practise being a good coach. Familiarise yourself with the coaching methods in this chapter, the exercises and drills in Chapter 4, the games in Chapter 5 and the coaching plans in Chapter 6, then go for it!

Starting up a club or team

First of all, you will need to find out where you can practise and improve your coaching skills. You may be able to join a tag rugby club either at a school or at community club level.

However, there are still lots of schools and places where tag rugby is not played. Rugby is such a great family sport that this is a real pity. If this is the position in your school or neighbourhood, why not start up a school or club tag rugby team? Through tag and mini rugby you can bring on your youngest players to junior and then senior rugby – and perhaps even academy status. This will ensure that professional rugby stars of the future are made. Wouldn't it be great to know that you originally coached the next Jonny Wilkinson as a mini player? However, it's not just about working towards stardom. Tag rugby is fun to play and, judging from the games that go on all week all over the country and the many competitions and tournaments, it's a great day out for all the family with the opportunity to watch a professional match and see some real international stars playing for their clubs.

If you want to start up a club of your own in the community from scratch, or if you want your club to join in such activities, contact your nearest senior club or the RFU. The RFU is a generous and committed supporter of community rugby and should be your first line of advice for both theoretical and practical tag rugby. Look on their website at www.rfu.com where you will find a wealth of information. You can also find the details of schools in your area from your local telephone directory and on your local council's website.

You can also create and manage your own Club Page website on the RFU Community Rugby site without the cost of domain names, hosting or special software. These Club Pages are very useful for communicating with other clubs and the information is also used in the RFU Yearbook, and the benefits of using them include:

- they're free to set up and use and reduce administration costs;

- your own club page can give your club the maximum exposure to potential new members – the postcode search tool on the RFU homepage links people directly to the clubs in their local area;

- they enable you to keep members up to date with your latest news and events;

- they allow you to display stories, match reports and photographs.

What's it like to be a club coach?

Jon Burton is Head Coach for tag rugby at Salisbury RFC. For Jon, coaching is about leadership, inspiring young people to excel and, above all, being great fun for the players. Rugby teaches fellowship, team spirit and accepting the word of the coach and referee.

Coaches need a keen eye to spot those beginning to struggle and those doing well, and it's always gratifying when a player moves up to a higher team. Jon likes being able to stay on the field during matches and truly loves to coach the Under 7s, but it must be remembered that the children's lack of maturity makes great demands in terms of patience, understanding and gaining and keeping attention and order. However, there's nothing Jon dislikes about coaching Under 7s. The weather doesn't bother him, although during really cold weather the club spends a lot of time keeping the children warm. The occasional parent will complain if they feel their child should be in a higher team, but Jon firmly but gently explains that he's the boss and makes the decisions.

Everyone likes to win, and so does Jon, but being part of the team is more important. The club puts on free meals for visiting teams and they have plenty of events, including race nights, discos, the Mini Tour at the end of the season and all sorts of entertainment for the children.

So, think carefully about why you want to be a coach. Are you prepared to do for others more than they do for you, prepared to learn, be patient, lead, inspire and motivate very young players in the game? If you are, don't hesitate. Find a club, become a tag rugby coach – and have a great time!

What next?

Next, you need to look around for a suitable place to train and play your matches. There are always plenty of public areas or senior pitches and clubs that will be willing to play host to tag rugby enthusiasts. You may even be able to use a local school's facilities. You can probably find all the information you need from the internet, your local library, council, newspaper and magazines or advertising cards in newsagents' windows for venues for your club. If this fails, place an advertisement of your own for somewhere to train.

If it has not already been done, be prepared to have your background checked by the police. This is legally required if you are going to work with children.

Basic equipment

Once you've got your venue you will need size 3 rugby balls, tags, tag belts, cones or markers for the pitch, a whistle if you wish and, of course, some players. All of you will need suitable sports clothing and sports shoes, or approved rugby boots, and the players will need mouth guards.

Sports kit doesn't have to be fancy and matching when you start out, but if you need help with providing kit there are many different ways of raising funds. Have a look at Chapter 9 for ideas on how to finance your club, apart from the subs you will need to charge each season to cover costs.

Help with coaching

It is always advisable to have at least one other adult or responsible older child with you, but having as many people as you can muster to help you will be a tremendous advantage. Having plenty of assistants will allow you to divide up the players into smaller groups and manage teams during a match. It is also a recommended safeguard in case of injury or accusation.

Adult parents or carers are usually the best bet. Some may be in a position to sponsor your club or school, so get them on your side. I've heard of dads who have sponsored the sports kit and even financed floodlighting. Also, some parents help out with the teams on the field as well as the coaches. It's perfectly acceptable for adults to be on the pitch helping the teams along at mini rugby level, and if an adult is available to oversee each team then the referee will have an easier job.

In a nutshell

- Familiarise yourself with the guidelines for working with children in Chapter 8.
- Find a suitable place to coach and play.
- Make sure you know the rules of tag rugby (see Chapter 2).
- Be familiar with how to coach and know the exercises, drills and games. Look at the RFU's website for initial help.
- Find enough players.
- Ensure you have the necessary equipment and sports clothing.
- Have fellow coaches or other adults to help you.
- Know your first aid and have a first-aid kit handy.
- Enjoy it!

Community rugby

Joining in with the professionals

Some professional clubs also make provision for tag rugby. For example, my club Harlequins, or Quins as they are known, have supported community rugby since 2000 when Chief Executive Mark Evans and Managing Director Tony Copsey arrived at the club. The *Richmond and Twickenham Times* newspaper is a committed sponsor and supported Quins' first cup tournament in 2001. Their involvement has enabled the match-day competition for 7–12 year-olds to develop into one of the most prestigious competitions in the south-east.

At each Quins home match there are 16 teams competing, which means the involvement of about 200 young players. The 7–9-year-olds play on the 1st XV team pitch and there are 60 clubs who have associate status at Harlequins. The under 7s are the tiniest of rugby players, but I've seen these little minnows playing tag rugby with heart and fervour, not to mention skill, on training days and in competitions at the prestigious Premiership clubs and National Division One clubs like Nottingham, Earth Titans (Rotherham), and Coventry – and, of course, at the Twickenham Stoop, the home of NEC Harlequins. It's a delight to see the visiting tag rugby teams playing on the main pitch before the professional game. Their families come to support them and everybody can then watch the big match in the afternoon. The tag teams at Harlequins form a guard of honour on the pitch at the start of the professional senior match and cheer on the visiting team – but then they erupt in even louder cheering and flag-waving for the Harlequins team when they run out. It's quite magical because the young players are very close to some of the biggest names in rugby, such as their heroes like Will

Greenwood (England international and World Cup winner), Andre Vos (a former South African international) and Andrew Mehrtens (the All Blacks legendary kicker). When the home side has run on to the pitch, the tag rugby players break away from their lines and charge at a furious pace off the field to their seats in the crowd, so excited to have been part of the professional senior game. It's a great day out for the family, ending with the opportunity to watch a professional match and see some real international stars playing for their clubs.

Some children also get to be a mascot for a match and run out onto the pitch with the team captain. Contact your local team, get a copy of their programme or search on the net for their website for details of how to become a mascot.

Find sponsorship too

One of the best ways to ensure that your club succeeds and flourishes is to find sponsorship. Most community programmes would not take place if they weren't sponsored. Sponsorship enables a very full season of competition and support. See Chapter 9 for further ideas about funding your club.

Make extra money for your club

Quins run a cash-back system that enables clubs to buy 10 match-day tickets for the price of 7. This means that a club can sell their free tickets and raise money for their club.

Find out where your nearest professional club is. They may run all sorts of activities, including community rugby and tag rugby competitions, which you can take part in. If they don't, why not have a go at persuading them? It will benefit them as much as it will you and your tag rugby team or club.

Maintaining discipline

When working with children it is essential to maintain discipline, earn their respect and not be too friendly, or they will take advantage of you and you may find yourself open to criticism or accusation. However, being too hard-line won't work either. Over-enthusiastic encouragement of your team to excel and win can lead to bullying the players. Don't let this happen to you. Maintaining discipline with children is always a delicate balance between keeping order and not being too regimented.

Keeping order is very important because ultimately the safety of all the children in your care depends on it. Also, in an orderly environment children are less likely to be bullied by other children and much more likely to enjoy themselves.

Encourage your players to say something nice, to look for the positive, or not say anything at all. You may think that calling a child names like 'fatso' or 'shorty' is harmless fun or will toughen them up, but such remarks can be deeply wounding. They are not appropriate and can undermine and upset a child who is sensitive about him- or herself.

If you feel a child is overweight, don't single him or her out with comments or actions. You may be able to help with a general emphasis on fitness and the desirability to eat healthily by speaking to all the children about fitness, but remember that young children have very little influence over how their lives are run. You may be able to discourage them from bringing unsuitable snacks and drinks to your coaching sessions, but you cannot lay down rules for what happens at home. You can, however, give a talk to the parents and carers about the relationship between a healthy diet and being fit so that they are aware of its importance. Gaining their co-operation is key to ensuring that the children in your care achieve fitness, not only through exercise but also through a healthy lifestyle.

Once you have established a really good relationship with the teams you are coaching you will be able to have a joke and engage in friendly banter and no-one will be offended. It will also encourage the children not to take you, themselves or the game too seriously.

Be firm but not harsh

You can often defuse a potentially bad-tempered situation with a bit of humour. If the players see you as grumpy and miserable, they won't co-operate. If the adults think you're a tyrant, you'll lose their co-operation and goodwill too.

Taking care
Don't expect to like all children
Children are the same as adults as regards their characters: they can be easy-going, shy, cheeky, bombastic, know-it-all, kind, unkind, caring and so on. Some you will naturally take to more than others, but you should try not to let this influence either the way you treat each child or the decisions you make. Children have an innate sense of fairness and will immediately spot favouritism or bias, but remember that they'll probably still grumble, however fair you are!

Parent power
Parents will have their opinions about who you choose for the team, especially if it's not their child. Parent pester power can be a nuisance, but you are in charge so don't be defensive. Explain the reason for your choice and stick to it. If you

have too many players for a team, you can rotate them and give each player a chance of playing. However, if you know you are doing the right thing you will have to learn to live with not being popular with all of the people all of the time.

Be firm about not tolerating interference or too much vocal encouragement from the adults on the sidelines and under no circumstances tolerate bad or abusive language of any nature (for example sexist or racist) from anybody, adults or players. People can get carried away with their passion; that's understandable. However, lack of respect, anger and intolerance all contribute towards an aggressive attitude that at its worst can spill over into violence. So nip it in the bud and encourage a good sporting attitude that will allow enthusiasm and support for a child or team, but not at the expense of a pleasant and safe atmosphere.

Give parents and carers a copy of the RFU's Good Parent's Code in Appendix 1. So far, rugby at all levels has remained largely unblemished by hooliganism among its supporters and there is no need for supporters of different teams to be in separate sections of the stadium at matches, nor for the supporters to be segregated and escorted to and from the match by the police. Despite all the fierce rivalry, and especially at the big internationals, you mix with the other supporters and congratulate the winners or commiserate with the losers after the match. Play your part in keeping it that way. After all, it's only a game.

Peaceful and polite

At the end of a Six Nations match between England and Scotland at Twickenham, I stopped to pat a police horse and was surprised to see that neither horse nor rider were wearing any protective gear. There were no shin guards or blinkers for the horse, and no faceguards and riot shields for the policewoman. When I expressed my surprise at this, she explained that at rugby matches it wasn't necessary because the supporters were peaceful and polite. That's fantastic. Let's all keep it this way!

A few principles

It can be very daunting to have a group of children to organise and coach effectively and safely for an hour or more. So remember a few principles:

- You're in charge. Make sure all the children are attentive and listen when you wish to speak to them. If you stand still and quiet yourself once you've called for them to be quiet, it will soon dawn on the chatterboxes that you are waiting. Do this for as long as it takes, but then tell the children that if they continue to talk when you've called for quiet you will apply a sanction.

- Let them know what you expect of them – no bullying and so on – and tell them that self-discipline is very important for sport in terms of safety, courtesy, improvement and enjoyment.

■ Tell them that if they have a problem of any sort they should come and tell you in confidence. Have a strategy for dealing with bullying of a physical, racist, or sexist nature.

How to tackle bullying

Encourage the children in your care to tell you if they are being bullied, and look out for it yourself. Be firm initially. Make it very clear that you will not tolerate such poor behaviour, but also try to understand why it is happening. Bullies have sometimes been bullied themselves and usually have a problem with self-image, so try to praise them and build up their confidence so they don't need to pick on others. Foster team spirit and encourage the children to help others in the team. Talk to all the children about this problem and get them on your side. It's cool to care.

Before the coaching session

Sensible measures for the players

Check the following before you start each coaching session.

■ No child to be wearing jewellery that is likely to cause injury to him- or herself or to another child.

■ Check footwear and clothing: are they suitable for your pitch conditions and the session itself?

■ Long hair: is it tied back safely?

■ Mouth guards: encourage all players to wear mouth guards. They don't just protect the teeth, they also protect the tongue, jaw and skull.

■ Have plenty of drinking water ready for half time. If children are allowed their own drinks, try to encourage them to choose sports drinks that contain the necessary carbohydrates (like sucrose and glucose) and electrolytes (sodium and potassium). These prevent dehydration and provide extra energy. They are more effective but also more expensive than water.

■ Healthy snacks: encourage the children to go for energy bars or cereal bars rather than crisps and chocolate containing colouring and additives, which may hype them up in the wrong way. If cereal bars are too expensive and you have a child or adult who loves cooking and has the time, you could ask them to make some flapjacks or similar cakes packed with energy and goodness.

The ground and surroundings

Check the following:

- Hazards such as glass or solid walls. Have a pair of heavy-duty gardening gloves and a strong bag handy for picking up any broken glass or drinks cans. Note whether there are any walls or fences close to play.

- Animal waste. This may be from dogs or foxes. While it is a legal requirement now to pick up after your dog, not all dog owners scoop so if you're playing on a public ground a good search of the playing area is advisable.

- Markings: are they clear and correct?

How to plan a coaching session

Running straight out on to a field to play a game of tag rugby is neither advisable from the exercise point of view or for sports safety, nor is it going to help improve your players' skills. A gradual build-up to a vigorous game of rugby will get the maximum out of your coaching session and will contribute to an enjoyable experience for the players. One way of planning a coaching session is as follows:

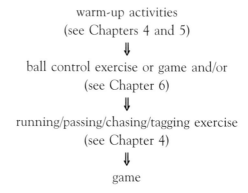

warm-up activities
(see Chapters 4 and 5)
⇓
ball control exercise or game and/or
(see Chapter 6)
⇓
running/passing/chasing/tagging exercise
(see Chapter 4)
⇓
game

Use the coaching plans in Chapter 6 to start yourself off and establish a routine. Whatever you're doing, don't forget to keep fun and enjoyment for the young players as top priorities. The more they enjoy your sessions, the more they'll co-operate with what you're trying to achieve, and the more you motivate them the better they'll play. This way everyone wins!

Remember that there are always marked physical differences in size, weight and height between children of the same age at junior school, so be prepared for this. Try to balance the difference in your teams and ensure that you pitch your exercises and drills at the correct level for the age of the children you're coaching and their experience of playing tag rugby. The coaching plans in Chapter 6 are graded and include exercises and games. They start with absolute beginners who have never played tag rugby before, while the last sessions consolidate what has been learned so that the players are prepared for a full game of tag rugby.

After the match or coaching session

After the match or coaching session, the children should perform some warm-down exercises (see Chapter 4). Then gather the players around and speak positively about the session. This will ensure a good sporting attitude and team spirit. Always praise the positive aspects of the game and let the players know that you will be practising any aspect of their play that needs improvement.

Have a drink together to rehydrate your body after vigorous exercise. Smoothies and yoghurts are excellent for replacing energy as the protein and carbohydrates in them will help glycogen recovery, but there's nothing wrong with a good drink of water. This also encourages a sense of being part of a team off the field. If everyone runs off and goes home straight after the game or session, you lose that club togetherness.

Finally, be prepared to enjoy what you're doing and make it exciting for the players too!

Negative can be positive

As a coach or teacher you will need to point out where improvements in team play and individual skills are needed, but this doesn't have to be a negative experience. 'A fantastic effort team, but next time we're going to see if we can win, aren't we?' 'That was good running, Peter, but don't forget to find space and side-step to avoid being tagged.' 'You tried really hard at tagging, Clare, and we'll all be able to have more practice at this in the next session/lesson.'

Before you move on to the practical side of tag rugby, have a look at the RFU Fair Play Codes in Appendix 1. They will help you, the players, assistants, spectators and match officials to participate in and observe the game in a spirit of understanding, positive encouragement, enjoyment and appreciation.

Be passionate

To be a coach you have to be really passionate about the game and love working with children. It can be very demanding and time-consuming, but it is always very rewarding and enjoyable.

4

4 | **exercises and drills**

You can combine the exercises and drills in this chapter with the games in Chapter 5 to make your own coaching sessions, following the structure outlined in Chapter 3 (see page 28). Alternatively, you can use the coaching plans in Chapter 6.

Warming up and warming down

Warming up exercises are important in any sport, for three reasons:

■ Learning or practising skills – the exercises in this chapter will help to develop the basic skills needed to play tag rugby and will improve play

■ Physical – the exercises gently stretch muscles, aid mobility, increase the flow of blood to the muscles and help prevent injury.

■ Psychological – the exercises prepare players mentally for the tasks ahead, improve concentration and encourage team spirit.

Begin gently or there is the risk of muscle strain. The whole object of warming up is to prepare the body for sustained energetic exercise, so the players need to work up to this in a controlled way. Mix exercises that are performed at a gentle jogging pace with those that can be done standing still.

When the players are warmed up, you can play any of the games in Chapter 5 or organise matches among the players.

Warming down lets the body recover gently from vigorous exercise:

■ Physical – the exercises allow the body to return to its normal resting state.

■ Psychological – the exercises calm the players down mentally.

Getting organised

All the exercises and drills in this chapter are designed to be done outdoors, but if the weather is bad they can be just as effective indoors providing there is enough space in a sports hall or club building.

The exercises can be done by both beginners and more experienced players because there are both simple tasks and harder, more complex tasks.

Equipment needed

■ One ball for each team of players.

■ At least 24 markers.

■ Bibs or bands for half the players.

■ One tag belt with two affixed tags per player.

Not enough cones?

If you don't have enough cones, ask the children to make markers for you with large cardboard circles about one metre in diameter and to colour them in bright colours. These markers will be just as effective as cones and are much cheaper. Obviously, if it is raining you will need to either laminate the paper markers or use plastic cones.

Marking out the pitch

Mark out grids and channels using lines and/or markers on the playing surface. The size of the grids should reflect the age and ability of the players and the type of activity being performed: for very young players, grids of 10 m × 10 m are sufficient.

Several grids can be joined to make larger areas by the removal of the central marker, which ensures quick movement throughout the session. (See Fig. 4.1(a).) Channels are formed by marking out a series of rectangles on the pitch. These are particularly good for practising passing in groups. (See Fig. 4.1(b).)

Figure 4.1(a) | Grid layout

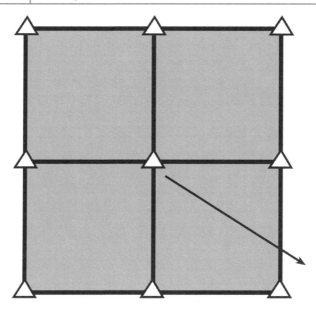

Figure 4.1(b) | Channels

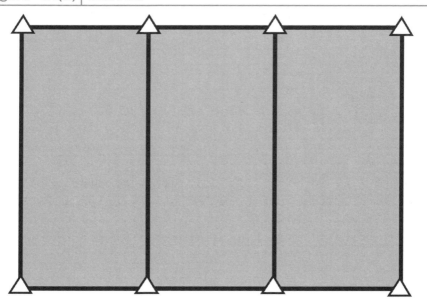

Mark them clearly

If you can, use different coloured markers for each grid or channel. This will help the players to see the boundaries for their playing area.

Coaching tips

- It is important, particularly if the players are new to tag rugby, that they hold a ball in both hands when performing these exercises so that they can practise running with the ball.
- Give clear instructions and demonstrations and ensure that all the players understand what to do.
- Ensure that the players get moving quickly and don't get cold or bored.
- Keep an eye on all the players and help out any group that is struggling.
- When suitable, introduce competition between teams or individuals to create an element of fun and interest.

Key to illustrations

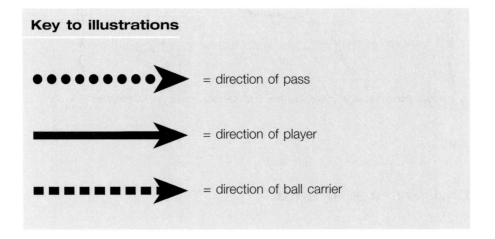

= direction of pass

= direction of player

= direction of ball carrier

Touch Ball

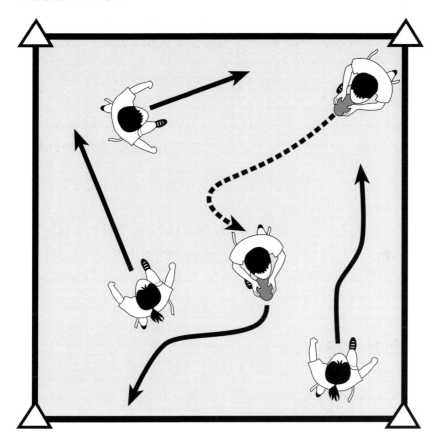

Aim

To develop running and evasion skills.

Equipment and setup

- Groups of 5
- 20 m × 20 m grid per team
- Size 3 ball per team

How to play

The ball carrier tries to touch as many players as possible with the ball. The other players look for space to run into and should not be closer than 1 m to the other runners. The ball carrier keeps count of the number of times players are touched with the ball. After 1 minute the teacher/coach calls 'Stop!' and the ball is handed over to another player.

Disabled children

If a child has very reduced mobility or is in a wheelchair, he or she can record who has received a touch ball and how often. Once a player has been touched by the ball, he or she has to report this to the disabled child. At the end of the game the players will know how successful they have been in this exercise.

Coaching tips

- The ball carrier must keep both hands on the ball at all times and touch the other players very gently.
- Encourage the players to look for space.
- Remind the players of the evasion rule and that they should dodge other players.

Variations

Easy

Reduce the dimensions of the grid.

Advanced

- Increase the dimensions of the grid.
- The touched player must be touched twice before the ball carrier moves on to another player.

Crossing the Channel

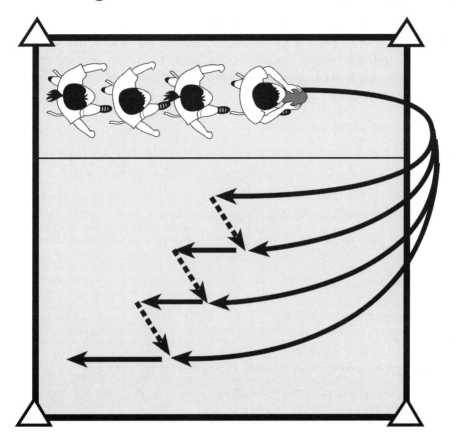

Aim

To develop running and passing skills and to work as a team at finding space.

Equipment and setup

- Groups of 4
- Two channels, one 20 m × 15 m and one 20 m × 5 m
- Size 3 rugby ball per group

How to play

The first team lines up behind the ball carrier at one end of the narrow channel. They run to the other end of the narrow channel then turn into the wide channel and fan out. The ball carrier passes to the player next to him or her, and so on along the line. As one team turns into the wide channel, the next team sets off.

Disabled children

If a child has very reduced mobility or is in a wheelchair, he or she can give the call for each team to start when the team in front has turned into the wide channel and the ball has been passed at least twice. This will allow the coach to concentrate on skills development.

Coaching tips

- In the narrow channel, the ball carrier should be told to get ahead so that he or she can change direction and slow down before delivering the pass.
- The others in the team should be told to try to keep within easy passing range of the ball carrier once they are in the wide channel.
- Encourage the ball carrier to look ahead when running but look at the other player's position and hands when passing.

Variations

Easy

Start with a run until the wide channel, where the players can slow down to a jog or even a walk if beginners.

Advanced

Add another player, or even two, to make teams of 5 or 6.

Conga

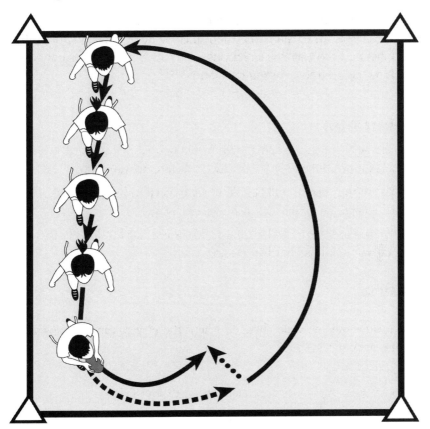

Aim

To develop skills for passing and support.

Equipment and setup

- Groups of 5
- 20 m × 20 m grid per group
- Size 3 ball per group

How to play

The ball carrier is the leader. The other players form a line behind. The ball carrier can run in any direction and the rest must follow. When the coach/teacher calls 'Pass!' the ball carrier must stop and hold out the ball to one side. The next player in line takes the ball and continues running in any direction as the new leader. The former ball carrier joins the back of the line.

Disabled children

If a child has very reduced mobility or is in a wheelchair, he or she can give the call for the ball carrier to pass. He or she can also call 'Change!' which means the ball carrier must change direction. This will allow the coach to concentrate on skills development.

Coaching tips

Encourage the players to:

- run into space
- follow the ball carrier
- leave a good space between players
- try to take the ball without slowing down.

Variations

Easy

Walk or jog.

Advanced

Change the method of passing the ball, for example placing the ball on the ground with both hands. It should be picked up with both hands. Alternatively, it could be passed in the normal way. These two methods could be sequential, with the call 'Ground!' then 'Pass two hands!' then 'Ground!' and so on.

Calling the Shots

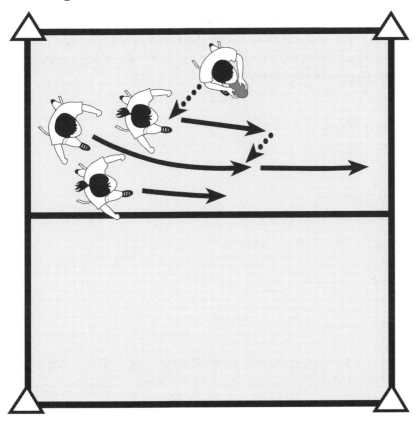

Aim

To develop running and passing skills and to work as a team.

Equipment and setup

- Groups of 4
- Two adjacent channels, each 20 m × 10 m
- Size 3 rugby ball per team

How to play

Three players fan out away from the ball carrier and run through the first channel. The last player in the team is the fourth player and receives the ball. The ball carrier must get him or herself in a position to pass, level or ahead of the other players. The ball carrier calls 'Pass!' The fourth player bursts through, gets into a position to receive the pass and calls for the pass. The team then runs on to the next channel and repeats the exercise.

Disabled children

If a child has very reduced mobility or is in a wheelchair, he or she can give the call for each group to start when the group in front has turned into the second channel and the ball has been passed again. This will allow the coach to concentrate on skills development.

Coaching tips

Encourage the players to:

- space out, not bunch together
- listen to the ball carrier's call for the pass.
- The support runner/receiver should find space and let team-mates know he or she is ready to burst through, then achieve explosive pace through the line of team-mates.
- The ball carrier should get into a position close to the receiver.

Variations

Easy

The first three attackers walk or jog slowly, and the fourth player can run once the call for the pass has been given.

Advanced

Add a defender who will try to tag the attackers.

It's a Try!

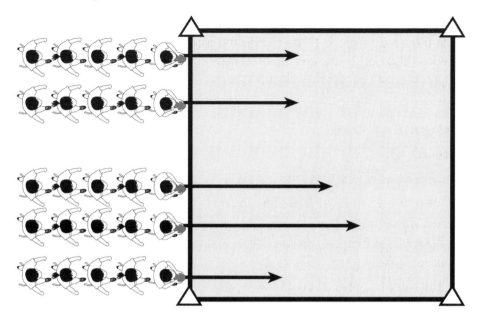

Aim

To develop individual ball skills in relays.

Equipment and setup

- Groups of 5
- Mark out a line 10 m from the start line.
- Size 3 ball per team.

How to play

Players line up in their teams behind the start line. The player at the head of the line is the ball carrier. The ball carrier runs to the 10 m line and back, performing skills along the way. The ball is handed over to the next player in line who performs a different set of skills and so on.

There are many possibilities with this exercise depending on the capabilities of the players, but some ideas for skills are as follows:
1. Run to the 10 m line and score a try, then run back and pass to the next player.
2. Pass the ball around the body twice while running to the 10 m line and back to the start line.
3. Throw the ball in the air and clap before catching it at the 10 m and start lines, then pass to the next player in line.

4. Ground the ball with both hands halfway across, then run to the 10 m line, turn and pick up the ball with both hands on the way back.

5. Run to the 10 m line, stop, raise one knee and pass the ball under that knee without dropping it. Repeat at halfway point on the way back.

Disabled children

If a child has very reduced mobility or is in a wheelchair, give him or her a list of the exercises and he or she can give the call for each player's drill as a reminder before the start. This will allow the coach/teacher to concentrate on skills development.

Coaching tips

■ Make sure that the players know which exercise they will be performing before the start. Demonstrate if necessary.

■ Keep teams small to maximise the activity.

■ When all five players have completed their ball-handling exercise, if there is time to repeat the exercise start at skill number 3 so the players all have a different task to do.

■ Perform the skills correctly: no cutting corners or the player has to go back and start again.

Variations

Easy

Choose one skill that all the players in the team perform.

Advanced

Apply a more difficult range of skills and have a time limit for each team to perform these skills.

Tag Attack!

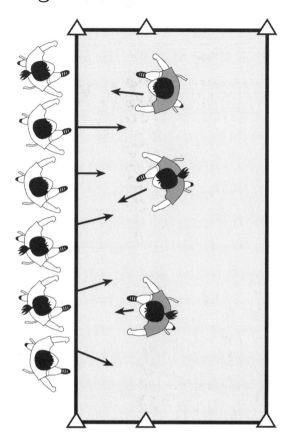

Aim

To improve evasion and tagging skills and to practise finding a space.

Equipment and setup

- Whole group together: divide players into attackers and taggers, with 1 tagger to 2 attackers
- Whole pitch: 60 m × 30 m
- Markers showing a 20 m position on the 30 m line
- All players wearing tag belts and tags

How to play

The attackers line up across the length of the pitch on the sideline with a 2 m gap between players. The taggers line up across the width of the pitch 20 m from their defence line. If there are lots of players, a second attacking team can be formed. On the coach/teacher's call of 'Go!' the attackers run towards the defence line, which is the opposite 60 m line. The taggers must try to tag as many of the attackers as they can. The attackers must run into space to avoid being tagged. When all attackers have reached the defence line, their tags are returned and the taggers resume their position on the 20m line. If there is another attacking team the players who have already run stay behind the defence line out of the way while this team runs. When all the attacking teams have had a run, start the drill again. After several turns the taggers can be swapped.

Disabled children

If a child has very reduced mobility or is in a wheelchair, he or she can give the call for each team to start. He or she can also keep a record of how many tags are taken on each run, which will show whether teams are improving with each run. This will allow the coach to concentrate on skills development.

Coaching tips
Encourage the attackers to:

- find space and avoid running into other players
- switch places on their subsequent turns so that the same taggers aren't targeting the same attackers each time
- keep a tally of how many times they're tagged.

Encourage the taggers to:

- select a target, keep their heads up and focus on the tag
- avoid running into other players
- select a different player as a target each time.

Variations
Easy
Have more taggers.

Advanced
Players drop out after being tagged twice. Tags are not returned until the end of the drill.

5

5 | fun and games

The games in this chapter are suitable for both clubs and schools, but for the benefit of schools they are related to the National Curriculum Key Stages 1 and 2. For more information about this, see pages 75–7.

General points

Tag rugby is played by very young children and the most important factor of the game is that they enjoy it, while also improving their fitness, developing all the necessary skills for team and competition levels and fulfilling the National Curriculum requirements. Drills and exercises can become very repetitive and lack the variety and action of games, where something different is happening all the time. Drills also lack group interaction, which helps to develop a sense of team spirit. Exercises and drills do have a place in tag rugby; indeed they are vital in improving fitness so that when a game is played the players do not tire before the end of the session or match. However, too much exercise of a particular kind can strain young muscles and put the players off. If it's seen as a drudge, they won't want to participate or they'll play reluctantly or badly. Fire them up with fun and games and they'll be bursting with enthusiasm!

Organisation

Before you begin a lesson or coaching session, be absolutely sure of how it is going to be organised and what you are going to do in the time allotted. This involves tailoring your activities to the playing area, the number of children in your class or club and the amount of time you have. Use the coaching plans in Chapter 4, or mix and match the activities as it suits you and as time allows. Before you start, ensure that the pitch is laid out and that you have all the equipment needed.

When children are running around enjoying themselves they don't always see problems, but if you organise them properly and they know that uncontrolled, boisterous behaviour can lead to injury, they will play safely. The players must learn to respond to your commands immediately. Not only is this a matter of establishing your authority, but it is also for their safety. When you blow your whistle and ask players to stop, insist that all the players cease activity, stand still and listen to you. Remind them of the rules, which do not allow barging or any other physical contact. Tagging involves only taking the tag. Neither the tagger nor the tagged player may fend off or pull at clothing to avoid or take a tag. See Chapter 2 for more on the rules of tag rugby.

A reward system can be helpful, with stars or similar being awarded for effort and achievement. If you're running a club, perhaps you can award a small prize to the player who has achieved the most at the end of the season. This does not have to be the best player: it can be the player who has made the best effort or the most progress.

Changing into sports kit

With very young children, changing into sports kit can take a long time and you may find that most of the session goes while they struggle to put their kit on. So it may be worth your while spending some time at the very beginning of your first session to concentrate on getting them to change quickly. Doing up sports-shoe laces can be a particular nightmare. Either get the children to wear shoes with Velcro straps or encourage them to learn how to tie laces for themselves as quickly as possible.

Spider's Web

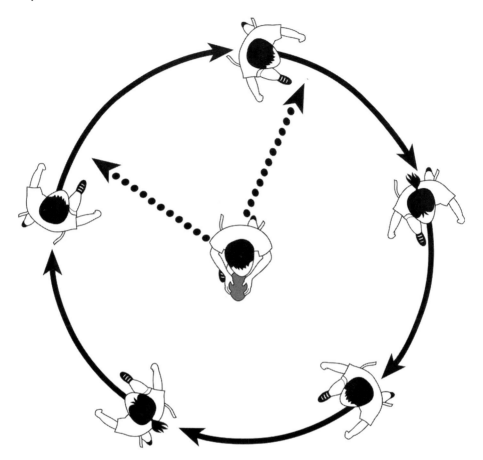

Aim

To improve ball passing and handling skills.

Equipment and setup

- Teams of 5 or 6 (this will depend on the space available – you can have as many players per team as your space allows, but more players will mean a bigger circle and players will be farther away from Spider.

- Size 3 rugby ball per team.

How to play

'Spider' is in the centre and the other players form a circle or web 2 m or more from Spider. Make sure there is a good space between each player making up the web. Spider stands still, holding the ball in both hands. When Spider shouts 'Go!' the other players start to run clockwise in a circle at a slow jogging pace. After a few seconds Spider shouts 'Stop' and the players stop running. Spider then passes the ball to the player who is either opposite or behind, but not in front, of him or her. That player catches the ball with both hands and passes back to Spider, who shouts 'Go!' again. Spider must pass to a different player each time. When

Disabled children

If you have a child who uses a wheelchair or has reduced mobility, this is an ideal game for his or her participation because the child can sit in a wheelchair or on a chair and be Spider. The ball can be passed and caught from this position. Once there is a change of Spider, and if the surface is suitable and there is a gentle walking pace, it may be possible for the child to join in with the other players to form the web.

Spider passes to the last player to catch a pass in any game, that player becomes the new Spider and the game restarts.

Coaching tips

Encourage players to:

- keep a good space between each other
- pass behind or across rather than forwards, but don't penalise absolute beginners who make forward passes
- stop if the ball goes to ground: all the players should wait until the ball catcher has retrieved the ball before starting to run again
- not make any jeering comments about a player who drops the ball or halts the flow of play in some way
- act in a sporting manner and adopt a good team spirit.

Variations

Easy

- Spider circles around on the spot while the players stand still. Spider shouts 'Pass' when ready to pass and must pass to a different player each time.
- As above, but the player who has caught the ball turns and passes it to the player behind him or her until all the players in the circle have had a chance to catch the ball. It is then passed back to Spider, who starts again.

Advanced
The players do not stop running when the ball is passed. The ball catcher passes back to Spider, who immediately passes to the next player, who passes back to Spider and so on. When all the players have caught the ball, the last to catch becomes the new Spider. With each new Spider the players run in the opposite direction from before.

Safety considerations
Each set of players must have sufficient room to move around. If space is limited, increase the number of players in each set. Alternatively, have only one Spider in the middle and all the players around in a circle. When a player has caught and passed the ball back to Spider, he or she drops out of that session and sits or stands quietly to one side.

If a ball is dropped, Spider shouts 'Stop!' and all players must immediately stop running until it is retrieved and held correctly in both hands. The game is then re-started.

If the playing surface is hard, you may consider that walking pace is more appropriate than running.

Scarecrow Tag

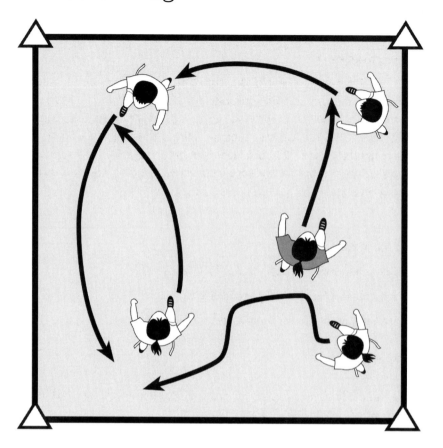

Aim

To develop running, tagging and evasion skills.

Equipment and setup

- Groups of 5
- 5 m × 5 m grid per group
- Tags
- Tag belts

How to play

One player is the defender, the other four are attackers. Players all find space and run in any direction, trying to avoid being tagged. The defender takes as many tags as possible: when a tag is taken, he or she calls 'Tag!' and must then hand back the tag. On the 'Tag!' call the tagged player must stand still, reaffix the tag and then stand still with arms outstretched. Another attacker must crawl under an arm of the tagged player to free him or her.

Disabled children

Scarecrow Tag may not be suitable for some children with reduced mobility. In this case, ask them to be the collector for the tags. The tagger must hand the tag to the collector, who will then hand it back to the tagged player. In the advanced version, two tags from the same player are collected before being handed back. The collector may also be able to keep score of the tags taken from individual players so that the players know how many times they've been tagged.

Coaching tips

- Attackers must keep their heads up and look for space.
- The defender should focus on the attacker's tag.
- Ensure that the tags are handed back and not thrown down.

Variations

Easy

Use a smaller grid. To free a tagged player, an attacker must run under the outstretched arms of the tagged player and shout 'Free!'

Advanced

The defender must remove both tags from the same attacker before moving on to a different player.

Weavers

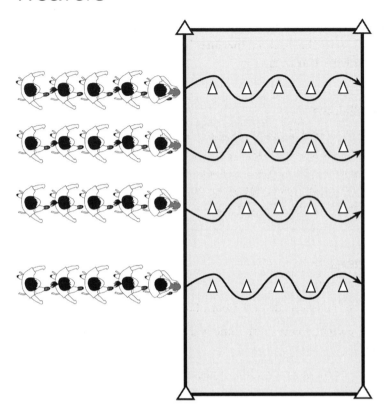

Aims

- To learn how to weave/side-step and avoid being tagged.
- To score a try.

Equipment and setup

- Groups of 5 or 6
- Markers placed across the pitch at regular intervals in a straight line for each group (use either the width of the pitch between the two sidelines or the length of the pitch between the two goal lines, depending on the age and ability of the players)
- Size 3 ball per team

How to play

Teams line up at the edge of the pitch. The leader holds the ball in both hands. When signalled to start, the leader starts to weave in and out of the cones with the ball in both hands. When he or she reaches the opposite line, the ball is grounded. The ball is then picked up by the same player and held in both hands while he or she weaves back to the start line and passes to the next player in line. The passer then goes to the back of the line. The action is repeated until all players in the team have had their turn.

Disabled children

Weavers is probably not suitable for children with reduced mobility, but you can assign them either to a particular team or the teams in general to watch out for infringements and alert the teams if an infringement has taken place. Let the players know that this is not about criticising their play, rather about being helpful in order for them to improve their play.

Coaching tips

Make sure that the players:

- hold and pass the ball correctly, using both hands

- ground the ball correctly beyond the line, staying on their feet, bending over and not diving

- weave in and out of the markers without missing any out, touching or running over them

- start again if there are any infringements.

- Allow one point for a successful try.

- Advanced players should keep a cone's distance between each other.

- Congratulate all teams and encourage them to finish faster and with fewer infringements next time.

Variations

Easy

Use fewer markers and/or have the markers more widely spaced.

Advanced

Have the cones closer together and set a time limit for the teams to finish within, and dock a point for any infringement. This score is deducted from the team's try score. When the teams play this game again they can aim for fewer dropped balls and more points.

Pass the Parcel

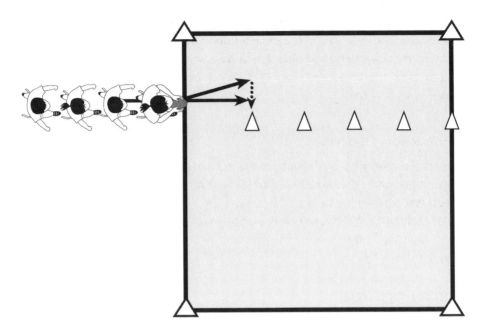

Aims

- To improve passing and support play.
- To learn how to take the ball on the run.
- To run 25 m carrying and passing the ball as a team.

Equipment and setup

- Groups of 5
- Markers showing 25 m line across the width of the pitch
- Markers for each corner of the pitch
- Markers spaced at 5 m intervals across the pitch for each team
- Size 3 ball per team

How to play

Teams line up in single file next to each other. The player at the head of each team carries the ball first. The ball carrier runs to the 5 m marker, stops, and holds out the ball for the next player to take. When the ball is held out, the next player in line runs to the ball carrier, takes the ball, runs on to the next 5 m marker and holds out the ball, and the next player then runs to take the ball and so on. The player who held out the ball should stay in position on his or her marker. The player next in line should begin running when the player in front reaches the first 5 m marker. The last player in the team should take the ball and score a try after reaching the 25 m line. When the game is finished, four players should be standing still by their markers and the fifth should have scored a try.

Repeat with the try scorer heading the team each time to give each player a chance to score a try.

Disabled children

A disabled child who cannot participate in Pass the Parcel could be assigned to a team, either to ensure that the ball is grounded correctly or to call 'Go!' when one player has reached the 5 m marker and it's time for the next player to begin the run. In the advanced version, this child could record the try score for a particular team.

Coaching tips

- Players must keep 5 m distance between each other.
- Remind the ball carriers to stop at the next 5 m marker and hold out the ball.
- Encourage the players to take the ball without slowing down or stopping.
- The last player always scores a try to finish the game.
- Award a point to the team that finishes first in each game.
- Congratulate all teams on their effort and encourage improvement for the games to follow.

Variations

Easy
Beginners could use a walking or gentle jogging pace instead of running.

Advanced
Instead of standing still at the marker after the ball has been taken, the player who has passed the ball runs to the back of the line and play is continuous for a set period of time. Note the team that has kept to the rules and scored most tries.

Bulldog Baggers

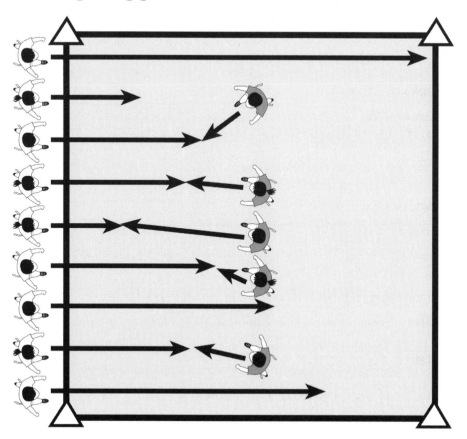

Aims

- To improve running and evasion skills.
- To improve defending and tagging skills.

Equipment and setup

- 30 m × 30 m grid, marked in the corners
- Tag belts
- Tags

How to play

Five players are defenders, the others are attackers. The five defenders, known as Bulldogs, are at the halfway point and fan out across the pitch. On the coach's call, the attackers try to run past the Bulldogs to the opposite side of the pitch without being tagged. The Bulldogs try to tag the attackers as they pass. Once tagged, that player joins the defenders as a Bulldog. When all the attackers who haven't been tagged have lined up again, and all the tagged players have taken up their positions at the halfway point, the coach starts the game again.

Disabled children

A disabled child who cannot participate in Bulldog Baggers could be assigned to ensure that the players keep to the rules and do not fend off, grab clothing or infringe in any other way. Alternatively, see the 'Easy' option below.

Coaching tips

- Encourage the attackers to look for space to run into to avoid being tagged.
- Encourage the Bulldogs to keep their heads up and select an attacker for tagging rather than rushing about aimlessly.
- All tags must be handed back after a successful tagging.
- Bulldogs should try to defend in one line as a team.

Variations

Easy

Attackers have to hop on one leg. This could enable those with limited mobility to take part as the pace of the game is much slower.

Advanced

- The same five players remain as Bulldogs and are not joined by tagged players. Once tagged, a player has to drop out of the game until the next game starts.
- Bulldogs have to tag the same player twice before they drop out of the game.

Run Rabbit Run

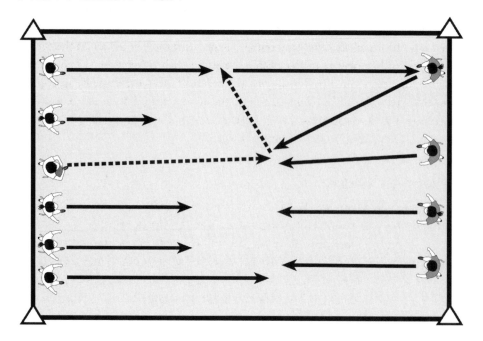

Aims

- For attackers to run into space, avoid being tagged and score a try for their team.
- To make the right decisions as regards where to run and who to pass to once tagged.
- To keep play flowing.
- Defenders can improve their tagging and defending skills.

Equipment and setup

- Groups of 10
- 30 m × 20 m pitch with markers at the 4 corners, a centre line and a 7 m line either side of the centre line
- Size 3 ball per team
- Tag belts
- Tags

How to play

Six attackers play against four defenders. The four defenders fan out across the width of the pitch at least 7 m from the centre line in the half of the pitch that they are defending. The attackers should fan out as a team, with the ball carrier on the centre line and the other players behind. Start the game with a free pass at the centre. The attacking team must try to run past the defenders to score a try. If tagged, the player must pass the ball backwards to a team-mate within 3 strides or 3 seconds. After a tag, the defender must hand the tag back and retreat to stay onside, and must not attempt to intercept or obstruct a pass.

Disabled children

A disabled child who cannot participate in Run Rabbit Run could be assigned to make the call for the first team, then the other teams in order, to line up in their positions ready for the game to start. When all players are in position, he or she can then start the game by calling 'Go!' He or she can also keep track of the number of tags taken and tries scored for each team. This will free up the teacher or coach to concentrate on ensuring that infringements do not occur. If they do, the teacher or coach can draw attention to the infringement so that players learn the correct way to play tag rugby.

Coaching tips

- The attackers must try to dodge the defenders.
- Pass if tagged, if about to be tagged or if a team-mate is in a better position.
- The ball carrier's team must stay behind the ball.
- The team should communicate with each other.
- The defenders should keep their heads up to concentrate on who to tag.
- Defenders should always hand the tag back after a successful tag.
- It may be helpful for the taggers to keep a tally of how many tags are made for each team.

Variations

Easy

Have seven attackers against four defenders.

Advanced

Have teams of 5 against 5, or 4 against 4.

6

6 | coaching plans

The following timed coaching plans, which use the drills and games in Chapters 4 and 5, can be used very effectively by both coaches and teachers. They last for either 30 or 60 minutes, or you can simply extract whichever exercises suit. However, remember to keep to the principles of warming up and warming down at the beginning and end of each lesson, coaching session or game. If you are not a teacher, go directly to Session 1 on page 65, missing out the National Curriculum notes.

The National Curriculum: Key Stages 1 and 2 for PE in England

The National Curriculum stresses the importance of physical education for pupils of all ages in schools. PE can involve a range of activities, including sports, and tag rugby meets the KS 1 and 2 requirements, which are: 'Physical education promotes physical skilfulness, physical development and knowledge of the body in action. It provides opportunities for pupils to be competitive and to face up to different challenges in groups and teams and it promotes positive attitudes towards active and healthy lifestyles.' It is important to note that getting involved in lifelong physical activity is encouraged from the outset and that tag rugby can be played very comfortably by 5-year-olds.

The following by no means contains the complete requirements and details of the National Curriculum, but it will give you an idea of what is expected of you as regards tag rugby. For full details, go to the government's website: www.gov.uk.

Key Stage 1
During this stage, pupils will be able to 'build on their natural enthusiasm for movement' and begin to 'work and play with other pupils in pairs and in small groups'. Tag rugby meets this requirement through exercises and in the team games.

Knowledge, skills and understanding
In this section the teacher needs to 'ensure that when evaluating and improving performance, connections are made between developing, selecting and applying skills, tactics and compositional ideas, and fitness and health.' Among the many

and varied skills to be acquired and developed by pupils in KS1, tag rugby can contribute in the following ways by teaching pupils to:

- remember and repeat simple skills and actions;
- use these skills and actions in sequence and combination;
- vary the way they perform skills by using simple tactics and movement phrases;
- describe what they have done;
- observe, describe and copy what others have done;
- appreciate how important it is to be active;
- travel with, send and receive a ball in different ways;
- use simple tactics for attacking and defending.

In tag rugby, beginners will be learning, developing and improving a whole range of skills, including running, ball control, hand–eye co-ordination, passing the ball, evasion tactics, working in pairs and being part of a team.

Key Stage 2

During this stage pupils will 'enjoy being active in physical activity. They learn new skills, find out how to use them in different ways and link them to make actions, phrases and sequences of movement. They enjoy communicating, collaborating and competing with each other. They develop an understanding of how to succeed in different activities and learn how to evaluate and recognise their own success.'

Knowledge, skills and understanding

This is the same as for KS1, but tag rugby can further contribute to KS2 by teaching pupils to:

- consolidate their existing skills and use new ones;
- perform actions and skills with more consistent control and quality;
- plan, use and adapt strategies and tactics for individual, pair, small-group and small-team activities;
- identify what makes a performance effective;
- suggest improvements based on this information;
- have a knowledge and understanding of fitness and health;
- realise how exercise affects the body in the short term;
- warm up and prepare appropriately for different activities;
- understand why physical activity is good for their health and well-being;

- understand why wearing appropriate clothing and being hygienic is good for health and safety;
- use skills and tactics suitable for attacking and defending;
- work with others to organise and keep games going.

Very young school children

If your class has very young children (under seven) and there are more than 20 of them, you will probably spend most of your time getting them changed! You may literally have only five or ten minutes of the lesson left. If this happens you will have to select just one activity from the coaching plans. I would suggest that you explain the game first, then concentrate on how to hold the ball correctly, pass it while standing still in pairs and pass it when running in pairs, and how to tag. Once these skills have been practised, you can use them in fun team games and they'll then be ready for a game itself.

How to use the coaching plans

Following are six photocopiable coaching plans for you to use. You will also be advised where to find more detailed information for the exercises, drills and games in these plans.

Note: if you use the 30-minute coaching plans for Sessions 1–3, you will need to use Sessions 1A and 2A in order to catch up with the skills covered in the 60-minute sessions. After this it is assumed that your players will know how to score a try, how to tag and how to pass, and you can therefore follow through from Session 4 onwards without having to use a 'catch-up' session.

The first session is particularly important as it introduces the children to the game for the first time. I'll therefore take you through this session in more detail to show you how the coaching plans work.

Session 1: absolute beginners
Tag rugby: what is it?
It is essential that the children know what tag rugby is and how they should play the game, so it will pay off if you spend time initially explaining the basic principles, using the rules in Chapter 2. It will also be very helpful to use some of the pupils to demonstrate what you are saying.

The object of the game is to score a try
Both hands on the ball, over the try line, no diving.

How to tag

It is essential that the players know how to wear a tag belt correctly and how to take a tag.

No tackling, kicking or contact of any kind

Explain that tag rugby for minis is not like midi or senior rugby to ensure that younger children do not get injured, but make sure they know how exciting this game can be.

Free passes

Explain why and how free passes are taken.

Warming up at the start

Begin gently or there is the risk of muscle strain or other injury. The whole object of warming up is to prepare the body for sustained energetic exercise. Therefore, the players need to work up to this in a controlled way. Mix exercises at a gentle jogging pace with those that can be done standing still, depending on the age and skills of the children.

Warming down at the end

Always end with a few minutes of warm-down if possible

Note: All sessions allow time for changing.

SESSION 1: Getting started

Duration: 30 minutes or 60 minutes

Objective: Players will learn how the game is played (30 min) and how to pass the ball (60 min)

Tip: Not much time? Cut the time spent on exercises and concentrate on developing ball-handling skills, standing still and running.

Activity	Equipment	Action	Teacher/coach notes
1. What is tag rugby? Explaining the game 15 min	■ Size 3 rugby balls ■ Tags and tag belts	Full class seated and concentrating; volunteers in pairs. Demonstrate the rules (see Chapter 2) using volunteers.	Test the children if time.
2. Warm-down (30-min session) or warm-up (60-min session) 5–10 min		■ Touch toes: 5 or 10 times ■ Side-step: ten leading with the right leg then ten leading with the left	Begin gently – no muscle strain. Repeat these two exercises if time.

End of 30-min session. For next session, go to Session 1A (page 80).

3. How to hold and pass the ball 5 min	Size 3 rugby balls	In pairs, standing still, players hold the ball in both hands and pass to their partner.	Throw the ball gently with both hands. Catch with both hands.
4. Game: Spider's Web (ball-passing skills) 10–15 min	Size 3 rugby ball per team	All play together, or in teams of 5 or 6. Spider is in the middle with the ball. The other players form a circle and jog around. When the Spider shouts 'Stop!' everyone stops running, the Spider passes to one of the players, who passes back to the Spider. Repeat.	See pages 59–61 for more information on Spider's Web. Stand still to pass, or vary the pace or vary the game: for example, the Spider can shout 'Pass!' and the players can catch the ball and pass it back without having to stop.
5. Warm-down 5 min max		■ Touch toes: keep legs straight, bend over and touch toes ■ Relax: lie down, relax all muscles and think of the best thing that's happened all week.	Remind the children that warming down is very important. A very quiet moment at the end of the session is good for self-discipline.

End of 60-minute session. For next session, go to Session 2 (page 81).

PHOTOCOPIABLE, ENLARGE 130% Tag Rugby © Jane Liddiard 2006, A & C Black Publishers Ltd.

79

SESSION 1A: Getting started

Duration: 30 minutes

Objective: Players will learn how to hold and pass the ball.

Tip: Not much time? Cut the time spent on exercises and concentrate on developing ball-handling skills, standing still and running.

Activity	Equipment	Action	Teacher/coach notes
1. Warm-up 5 min max		■ Swing around: stand still with arms outstretched and swing arms around from side to side ■ Gentle jog around field of play, large or small area	Make space. Keep legs still and move upper body gently – don't twist your back.
2. How to hold and pass the ball 5 min	Size 3 rugby balls	In pairs, standing still, players hold the ball in both hands and pass to their partner.	Throw the ball gently with both hands. Catch with both hands.
3. Game: Spider's Web (ball-passing skills) 10–15 min	Size 3 rugby ball per team	All play together, or in teams of 5 or 6. Spider is in the middle with the ball. The other players form a circle and jog around. When the Spider shouts 'Stop!' everyone stops running, the Spider passes to one of the players, who passes back to the Spider. Repeat.	See pages 59–61 for more information on Spider's Web. Stand still to pass, or vary the pace or vary the game: for example, the Spider can shout 'Pass!' and the players can catch the ball and pass it back without having to stop.
4. Warm-down 5 min		■ Pedal power: lie on back and pedal legs in the air ■ Relax: lie down, relax all muscles and think of the best thing you've read this week.	Try to make a big arc with your feet. A very quiet moment at the end of the session is good for self-discipline.

End of session. For next session, go to Session 2 (page 81).

SESSION 2: How to tag

Duration: 30 minutes or 60 minutes

Objective: Players will learn how to tag and practise ball carrying.

Tip: Not much time? Cut the time spent on exercises and concentrate on how to tag.

Activity	Equipment	Action	Teacher/coach notes
1. Warm-up: Figure of Eight (ball-carrying practice) 5–10 min	■ Size 3 rugby balls ■ Tags and tag belts	Three players stand in a line; one player has a ball. Ball carrier jogs/ walks gently in a figure of eight around the other two players then passes the ball to player 2. Repeat with players 2 and 3.	Avoid touching other players. Carry the ball in both hands. Learn how to weave and avoid being tagged. Repeat until time's up.
Weavers (avoid being tagged) 5–10 min	■ Size 3 rugby balls ■ Markers in a straight line across the pitch at regular intervals	Teams of 5 or 6, one ball per team. Ball carrier weaves in and out of the markers, scores a try at the end of the line of markers, weaves back through the markers and passes to the next in line, who then performs the drill.	See page 64 for more information on weavers. Hold the ball in both hands and ground the ball correctly. No touching the markers – start the drill again if there are any infringements.
2. Tagging (learn how to tag) 10 min	■ Tags and tag belts	In pairs, one player steps forwards, takes partner's tag, holds it up and shouts 'Tag!' Continue until both tags of each player have been taken and reaffixed. Then practise running and taking the tag.	Tag belts to be worn correctly. Players to stand a few paces opposite partner. Only the defenders to take tags.
3. Warm-down 5 min max **If you are using the 60-minute coaching plan, miss out this stage and go to step 4.**		■ Touch toes: 5 or 10 times ■ Relax: lie down, relax all muscles and think of the best thing you've read this week.	Begin gently, no muscle strain. A very quiet moment at the end of the session is good for self-discipline.

End of 30-min session. For next session, go to Session 2A (page 83).

SESSION 2: How to tag Cont.

Activity	Equipment	Action	Teacher/coach notes
4. Game: Scarecrow Tag (running, tagging and evasion skills) 15 min	■ Tags and tag belts ■ Markers marking out 5 m × 5 m grids.	All play together, or in teams of 5. One player is defender/tagger, the others run to avoid being tagged. When the defender takes a tag, he/she calls 'Tag!' and then hands the tag back. The tagged player stands still, arms outstretched, until another player crawls under an outstretched arm.	See pages 62–3 for more information on Scarecrow Tag. Defender should focus on the attacker's tag. Attackers must keep their heads up and look for space. Tags must be handed back, not thrown down.
5. Warm-down 5–10 min		■ Gentle jog around field of play, large or small area ■ Swing around: stand still with arms outstretched and swing arms around from side to side	Keep legs still and move upper body gently – don't twist your back.

End of 60-min session. For next session, go to Session 3 (page 84).

SESSION 2A: How to tag

Duration: 30 min

Objective: Players will practise and improve tagging skills.

Tip: Not much time? Cut the time spent on exercises and concentrate on how to tag.

Activity	Equipment	Action	Teacher/coach notes
1. Warm-up 5–10 min		Gentle walk or jog	Tailor the pace and area to the age and fitness of the players.
2. Game: Scarecrow Tag (running, tagging and evasion skills) 15 min	■ Tags and tag belts ■ Markers marking out 5 m × 5 m grids.	All play together, or in teams of 5. One player is defender/tagger, the others run to avoid being tagged. When the defender takes a tag, he/she calls 'Tag!' and then hands the tag back. The tagged player stands still, arms outstretched, until another player crawls under an outstretched arm.	See pages 62–3 for more information on Scarecrow Tag. Defender should focus on the attacker's tag. Attackers must keep their heads up and look for space. Tags must be handed back, not thrown down.
3. Warm-down 5 min		Swing around: stand still with arms outstretched and swing arms around from side to side.	Keep legs still and move upper body gently – don't twist your back.

End of session 2A. For next session, go to Session 3 (page 84).

PHOTOCOPIABLE, ENLARGE 130% Tag Rugby © Jane Liddiard 2006, A & C Black Publishers Ltd.

SESSION 3: How to score a try

Duration: 30 minutes or 60 minutes.

Objective: Players will learn how to score a try.

Activity	Equipment	Action	Teacher/coach notes
1. Warm-up: Conga (passing and support play skills) 5 or 10 min	■ Size 3 rugby balls ■ Markers marking out a 20 m × 20 m grid	Teams of 5 in a line, one ball per team. Ball carrier leads and can run in any direction; the other players follow. When coach calls 'Pass!' ball carrier passes to the next player. Passer goes to the end of the line and the new ball carrier leads. Continue.	See pages 47–8 for more information on the Conga. Run into space, avoiding other teams. Follow the ball carrier and leave a good space between players. Catch the ball without slowing down.
2. How to score a try 15 or 20 min	■ Size 3 rugby balls ■ Tags and tag belts	Pairs of teams with up to five players per team line up on opposite side-lines. Ball carrier starts at the front of one line, and runs to the player at the head of the opposite line, grounds the ball with both hands and goes to the back of the line. Next player picks up the ball and runs to ground it on the opposite team line. Continue.	See pages 13–5 for more information on how to score a try. Hold the ball firmly in both hands. Ground the ball with two hands and both feet on the pitch. Ensure that all players have the chance to ground the ball at least once.
3. Warm-down 5 min **If you are using the 60-minute coaching plan, miss out this stage and go to step 4.**		■ Pedal power: lie on back and pedal legs in the air ■ Relax: lie down, relax all muscles and think of the best thing you've read this week.	Try to make a big arc with your feet. A very quiet moment at the end of the session is good for self-discipline.
End of 30-min session. For next session, go to Session 4 (page 86).			
4. Game: Weavers (skills to avoid being tagged) 15–20 min	■ Size 3 rugby ball per team ■ Markers in a straight line across the pitch at regular intervals	In teams of 5 or 6, the ball carrier weaves in and out of the markers to score a try, then weaves back and passes to the next player in line, who then performs the drill. Continue.	See page 64 for more information on weavers. Players will learn how to hold, ground and pass the ball correctly with both hands. No touching or running over the markers.

SESSION 3: How to score a try Cont.

Activity	Equipment	Action	Teacher/coach notes
5. Warm-down 5 min		Swing around: stand still with arms outstretched and swing arms around from side to side.	Keep legs still and move upper body gently – don't twist your back.

End of 60-min session. For next session, go to Session 4 (page 86).

SESSION 4: Let's play tag rugby!

Duration: 30 minutes or 60 minutes.

Objective: Evasion practice and a game.

Tip: Lack of time? Warm up for 5 min then go directly to step 3, missing out step 2.

Activity	Equipment	Action	Teacher/coach notes
1. Warm-up: Crossing the Channel (evasion, running and passing skills) 5 or 10 min	■ Size 3 rugby ball per team ■ Markers marking out two channels: one measuring 20 m × 5 m	Teams of 4. First team run after the ball carrier through the narrow channel and into the wider channel, then fan out and pass the ball along the line. The next team follow when the team ahead is in the wide channel.	See pages 45–6 for more information on Crossing the Channel. Ball carrier should look ahead when running and get ahead of his team while in the narrow channel to prepare for the pass. All players should keep within easy passing range. Look at the players' position and hands when passing.
2. Let's play tag rugby! 15 or 25 min	■ Size 3 rugby ball per team ■ Tags and tag belts ■ Bibs or different coloured tags for each team	In teams of 4, 5, 6 or 7 (same number of players in each team), play a game of tag rugby.	Remind children of the basic rules and how to play. Switch players around if any team is 5 points or more ahead to even out play. If you have only one teacher or coach for more than 14 players, give two teams a 5-min game while the others watch (if it's not too cold) or play one of the games in Chapter 5. Then swap the players around so everyone gets the chance of a game with the coach.
3. Warm-down 5 or 10 min		■ Swing around: stand still with arms outstretched and swing arms around from side to side ■ Pedal power: lie on back and pedal legs in the air	Go gently after all that action.

End of session. For next session, go to Session 5 (page 87).

SESSION 5: Improving skills

Duration: 30 minutes or 60 minutes.

Objective: To practise running and passing skills, working as a team and playing a game.

Tip: Lack of time? Warm up for 5 min, then choose either step 2 or step 3.

Activity	Equipment	Action	Teacher/coach notes
1. Warm-up: Calling the Shots (running and passing skills, working as a team) 5 or 10 min	■ Size 3 rugby ball per team ■ Markers marking out 2 adjacent channels, each measuring 20 m × 10 m	Teams of 4. In the first channel, players fan out from the ball carrier who calls 'Pass!' fourth player bursts through for a pass; when he or she is in position, calls 'Pass!' for the ball to be passed. Repeat in next channel.	See pages 49–50 for more information on Calling the Shots. Make sure the players understand the game. Players should burst through to receive the pass at pace. Find space and don't bunch together. Listen to 'Pass!' calls.
2. Game: Pass the Parcel (passing and support play) 10 min	■ Size 3 rugby ball per team ■ 5 markers placed in a straight line at 5 m intervals	Teams of 5 in a line. Ball carrier runs to first marker and holds out the ball. The next player takes it, runs with the ball to the second marker and holds it out for the third player, and so on. The first player goes to the back of the line. The fifth player scores a try. Award a point to the team who finishes first.	See pages 66–7 for more information on Pass the Parcel. Players must keep 5 m between them. At each marker the ball is held out for the next player. Congratulate all the teams on their effort and improvement.
3. Let's play tag rugby! 15 or 25 min	■ Size 3 rugby ball per team ■ Tags and tag belts ■ Bibs or different coloured tags for each team	In teams of 4, 5, 6 or 7 (same number of players in each team), play a game of tag rugby.	Remind children of the basic rules and how to play. Switch players around if any team is 5 points or more ahead to even out play. If you have only one teacher or coach for more than 14 players, give two teams a 5-min game while the others watch (if it's not too cold) or play one of the games in Chapter 5. Then swap the players around so everyone gets the chance of a game with the coach.

PHOTOCOPIABLE, ENLARGE 130% Tag Rugby © Jane Liddiard 2006, A & C Black Publishers Ltd.

SESSION 5: Improving skills Cont.

Activity	Equipment	Action	Teacher/coach notes
4. Warm-down 5 or 10 min		■ Pedal power: lie on back and pedal legs in the air ■ Relax: lie down, relax all muscles and think of the best book you've read recently	Try to make a big arc with your feet. A very quiet moment at the end of the session is good for self-discipline.

End of session. For next session, go to Session 6 (page 89).

SESSION 6: Further skills development

Duration: 30 minutes or 60 minutes

Objective: To practise running, evasion and tagging skills and finding space.

Tip: Lack of time? Warm up for 5 min, then choose either step 2 or step 3.

Activity	Equipment	Action	Teacher/coach notes
1. Warm-up: Bulldog Baggers (defending tagging, running and evasion) 5 or 10 min	■ Tags and tag belts	Use the size of pitch you normally play on. five children are Bulldog Baggers (defenders) and the rest are attackers. Bulldogs try to tag attackers; once tagged, players become Bulldog Baggers.	See pages 68–9 for more information on Bulldog Baggers. Players should look for space to avoid being tagged. Taggers should select a target – no aimless running.
2. It's a try! (multi-skills development) 5 or 15 min	■ Size 3 rugby ball per team ■ Markers marking out a line 10 m from the start line	Teams of 5 line up behind the start line. Ball carrier runs to the 10 m line and back while performing skills as directed by the coach, then passes the ball to the next player who repeats the drill.	See Chapter 4 for ideas on exercises and drills. Demonstrate the exercises and make sure players know which exercises they are doing.
3. Tag Attack (evasion and tagging skills, finding space) 10 or 15 min	■ Tags and tag belts ■ Markers marking out a 20 m line on a 60 m × 30 m pitch	One tagger to two attackers. Attackers run to the 20 m line and try to avoid being tagged. Another team of attackers can be waiting to start.	See pages 53–4 for more information on Tag Attack. Taggers should keep their heads up, select a target and focus on the tag. Attackers should look for space to avoid the tagger.
4. Warm-down 5 or 10 min		■ Pedal power: lie on back and pedal legs in the air ■ Relax: lie down, relax all muscles and think of the best TV programme or film you've seen recently	Try to make a big arc with your feet. A very quiet moment at the end of each session is good for self-discipline. No talking!

End of session.

7

7 | refereeing

Where to start

So you've always wanted to be a referee, or maybe you have to be a referee because your school or club needs you: where do you start? Rugby's a complicated game and if you haven't refereed a game of rugby before you may be worrying about the dizzying aspect of the rules in the professional game, but there's no need – tag rugby is really simple by comparison.

Naturally, before you can run out on to the field of play with whistle and notebook in hand, you will need to enrol for one of the Mini Referee courses developed by the RFU. Look up the next course in your area for the National Foundation Certificate as this is the first step on the refereeing qualifications ladder. Also, contact the Rugby Referee Development Officer in your area. You'll find all this information in the Referee section on the RFU website (www.rfu.com).

You will need to familiarise yourself with the rules (see Chapter 2) and make sure you know them thoroughly. There's no time for hesitation in a running game: you have to make decisions quickly and correctly, which means you have to be absolutely sure of what you are doing as a referee. As time goes on, your experience will give you more confidence and enable you to relax and enjoy the games.

One point you can be sure of, which will help if you feel nervous, is that you will always know more than the players at this level. Show confidence and authority and explain your decision by referring to the rules and everything should go well. Also, it stands to reason that the more games you referee the easier it will become.

You don't have to be old to be a referee

While watching a game of tag rugby at the Twickenham Stoop, home of the NEC Harlequins, I was impressed by the refereeing of Will Finlayson. Will is a young man – 22 years old – and has clearly attained a high standard. He did his work experience at Quins while still at school and this led to an interest in refereeing, as well as a great love of the club. He took the RFU's course and on the day I saw him he was refereeing six matches. Will was fair in his judgements and spotted infringements, but also allowed the game to flow. Young people from 14 years of age can become tag rugby referees. Find out how from this book and from the RFU's website.

You mean I can enjoy being a referee?

Absolutely! It all depends on you and your attitude. Admittedly, it's a big responsibility because the result, the flow of the game and the spirit in which it's played depends on your expertise, your interpretation of what's going on and your decisions. You may also be the subject of a little heckling from the sidelines or even some dissent from the players, but don't let any of that put you off. Being an efficient professional, and above all enjoying what you're doing, is really worthwhile because you are giving something to the young children of this country. All too often children get a terrible press and we only hear about their bad behaviour, but if the majority of children were uncontrollable, aggressive and worthless there would be complete chaos both in school and out of it. This does not happen. The majority of children are keen to learn and love participating in sports. If you love the game passionately it will inspire children.

Add to this the opportunity to travel to new venues, both locally and nationally, and to make new friends in the game and you'll understand how much you will get out of being a community referee.

Is it difficult to referee?

Sometimes, especially when you first start out. However, there is a lot of help available from local Referee Societies. If you have played the game you will already have knowledge of what is required and one enormous advantage is that you will know what it's like to be a player, which means you'll be able to empathise with your young charges. As you become more experienced, the science and art of refereeing become easier. Nevertheless, every match presents you with a challenge as no two matches are the same.

Support

Referee Societies have monthly meetings throughout the season where aspects of Law and refereeing management are discussed. The RFU also has a development pathway for Referees, Touch Judges, Assessors and Referee Coaches. Each step along the pathway is supported by an Award course.

So, your very first priorities are to:

- complete an accredited course for referees
- learn the rules of the game thoroughly (see Chapter 2).

Refereeing a game

Equipment needed for refereeing tag rugby

You won't need a suitcase for the equipment needed to referee a game of tag rugby but there are, of course, some essentials:

- whistle – and you may need a second as a back-up
- stopwatch – make sure you've practised with it before a match
- notebook or paper for keeping the score
- pen or pencil for recording the score and anything else of consequence that may happen during a game
- different coloured sports shirt from either team playing
- suitable sports shoes matched to the conditions of the playing surface. These will include trainers with good grip on the soles for hard surfaces, which may be dry impacted grassy areas as well as concrete or tarmac, and IRB-approved rugby boots for softer surfaces such as a playing field.

What to do before play begins

Check:

- the playing area: is it safe and free from any debris or animal waste?
- the pitch: is it within the width and length dimensions as laid out in the rules (see page 6) and are the lines clearly marked?
- the rugby ball: is it the right size? Do you need spares?
- the players: are there the same number of players in each team?
- watches and jewellery: ask the players to remove any items that could cause injury either to the player him- or herself or to other players
- shirts and tops: are they tucked securely into tracksuit bottoms or shorts?
- tags and belts: are the belt straps tucked in securely? Are the tags themselves hanging freely and not wrapped around the belt so they can be removed easily?

- mouth guards: these are always advisable, but the RFU insists on players having this protection in competitions. Encourage your players to be safe.

Problems?

Odd number of players

If you are a coach and also have to referee the game, and you find that you have an odd number of players, discuss this with the children and suggest that one of them helps you referee by becoming a touch judge for the first half of the game. This player could then swap with another player in the team for the second half. At least this way the extra player gets to play some of the time.

If there is no volunteer for this, ask the children to write their names on a piece of paper and fold it over. Put all these names into a container, give it a good stir and then draw out two pieces of paper. The first name out plays in the first half, the other is a touch judge and they change over for the second half.

Someone's not got the right kit

You will have to assess whether this child can play in what they have got. If you consider their clothing or footwear to be a safety issue you must not allow them to play, but if it's simply a matter of not having expensive trainers or not having the same kit as the others, there's no reason why the child cannot play.

Dissent and abuse of the referee

Dissent is when a player argues with the referee over a decision. This isn't likely to occur in a threatening or really serious manner by tag rugby players and abuse is more likely to come from the spectators, but it should always be nipped in the bud. Being a good sport is essential and arguing with decisions should not be tolerated at any level, even if that decision appears to be wrong. Encourage players to accept decisions gracefully and get on with the game. This can be reinforced when you are discussing the game of tag rugby with your players, or after a game, or on a bad weather day when you can't get a game going.

There are rare cases of abuse, but the RFU and Constituent Bodies penalise very heavily any player or club member shown to be abusive. All clubs have to agree to abide by the Code of Conduct for stopping the abuse of Match Officials (see Appendix 1).

Officials must always report in writing, to the Club or CB (Constituent Body) Welfare Officer and/or Society Secretary, behaviour by adults that you feel contravenes RFU Child Protection Policy (see pages 101–2 for more information on this). This may include the following:

- verbal bullying by coaches/parents/spectators
- physical abuse by coaches/parents/spectators

- inappropriate or aggressive contact by an adult to a young person
- verbal abuse directed at the official by young people or adults.

Remember: the welfare of all young people is paramount.

Starting the game

If you have time before the match, gather the teams together and tell them how you expect them to behave:

- keeping to the rules
- no bad language
- no taunting or laughing at any other player
- accepting the referee's decision without backchat
- 7-metre rule
- reversing decision for dissent
- being a gracious winner and a good loser.

Also remind them about finding space and keeping to their positions.

During the game

You should concentrate on:

- giving clear signals
- scoring properly
- forward passes
- correct tagging
- free pass rules
- dead ball
- knock on
- offside
- dealing with injury
- dealing with difficult players
- time keeping.

Dealing with problems

Always blow your whistle to stop play and explain briefly and to the point why you are doing this and what the infringement is for. Watch out for the following:

- bad language – give a warning at first, then an on-pitch penalty (free pass) for the next offence
- foul play – make it clear you will not accept this and why it is unacceptable, concentrating on safety and being a good sport, then award a free pass to the other side.

Punishing dissent in the senior game

In senior rugby, if a player argues with a decision made by the referee, the referee may move the penalty spot 10 m forward as a further punishment for dissent. This can mean the difference between having to kick for a line out or being able to kick for a penalty goal, worth three points. It is very effective and virtually eliminates insults or arguments about the decision.

At the end of the game

Gather the players around, remind them of the score and congratulate the winners, but also praise both teams. Get the players to shake hands with the opposing team and then ask the winning team to form a tunnel so that they can applaud the losing team off the field; this will encourage good sporting behaviour.

8

8 guidelines for working with children

Working with children is always very challenging and very rewarding, but if you are a coach, referee or any person involved in tag rugby, whether on a professional or volunteer basis, then you are obliged by law to provide those children with the highest possible standard of care.

This chapter contains essential information on the legal and moral requirements for anyone wishing to become involved with tag rugby, based on the RFU's own guidelines. The complete text of the RFU, RFUW (Rugby Football Union for Women) and the NSPCC's *Policy and Procedures for the Welfare of Young People in Rugby Union* can be found on the RFU's website (www.rfu.com) and you can download a copy for your own use. The RFU is very careful to ensure that these guidelines are understood and carried out. Although this may seem to be a common-sense matter, it isn't until you start looking at the issues that you realise there's much more to it than you think.

In its introduction to *Policy and Procedures for the Welfare of Young People in Rugby Union*, the RFU/RFUW states that:

- it is the responsibility of every adult working in rugby union, whether as a professional or a volunteer, to ensure that all young people can enjoy the sport in a safe and enjoyable environment;

- they recognise their responsibility to safeguard the welfare of all young people involved in the game by protecting them from physical, emotional or sexual harm and from neglect or bullying of any kind;

- they are resolute in meeting their obligation to ensure that all those clubs and schools providing playing opportunities for young people do so to the highest possible standards of care, whether in a paid or voluntary capacity.

However, the RFU knows that any procedure for children's welfare and protection is only as effective as the ability and skill of those who operate it. The RFU/RFUW are therefore committed to effective recruitment and appropriate training for all their coaches, volunteers and club members. This will enable them to work together with parents/carers and other organisations to ensure that the needs and the welfare of young people remain paramount.

This is the RFU's own policy to do all it can to protect young children and to ensure that its coaches, trainers, and volunteers understand and carry out this policy. This means you. The RFU's policy recognises that you are at the sharp end and that protecting and looking after children in a positive and enjoyable way can only work if you play your part.

So what does my school or club have to do?

Schools will have their own measures for dealing with child protection, but there's no reason why teachers shouldn't check out the measures below and compare them with their own school's policy. If you are a coach and starting up a club, or even if you're an established club, you need to:

- read, understand and act upon what's in this chapter;

- if practical and possible, appoint a Welfare Officer who will act as the first point of contact for concerns about the welfare of young people (see Appendix 2 of the RFU's Guidelines for 'Terms of Reference');

- accept that all officers and committee members have a responsibility in this area and be prepared to respond to any indication of poor practice or abuse;

- put in place structures and systems to ensure that this is followed in practice;

- adopt and implement a 'best practice' policy for all adults working with young people (see the Fair Play Codes in Appendix 1);

- ensure that all relevant members who have regular supervisory contact with children or a management responsibility for those working with young people undertake a Criminal Records Bureau disclosure (visit www.crb.gov.uk for more information).

What to look out for?

Emotional abuse

In a rugby situation, emotional abuse may occur when coaches:

- provide repeated negative feedback: 'I see you played like a drain as usual, Johnny.' 'If you pass like that in our games, Donna, we'll lose all of them.'

- repeatedly ignore a young player's efforts to progress: 'She's not worth helping. She'll never get any better.'

- repeatedly demand performance levels above those of which the young player is capable: 'you'll stick at this until you get it right.'

- over-emphasise the winning ethic: 'I don't want to see any losers in my teams. We're here to win.'

Abuse by neglect

In a rugby situation, neglect may occur when:

- young players are left alone without proper supervision;

- a young player is exposed to unnecessary heat or cold without fluids or protection;

- a young player is exposed to an unacceptable risk of injury.

Physical abuse

In a rugby situation, physical abuse may occur when coaches, managers or helpers expose young players to:

- exercise or training that disregards the capacity of the player's immature and growing body;

- overplaying, overtraining or fatigue.

Sexual abuse

In a rugby situation, sexual abuse may occur when the close proximity of coaches and others to young people provides opportunities for potential abusers to exploit their position of trust to sexually abuse.

Poor practice

Poor practice includes behaviour that contravenes any of the following:

- Fair Play Codes (see Appendix 1)

- Good Practice in the Rugby Setting (contained in *Policy and Procedures for the Welfare of Young People in Rugby*)

- Welfare and Procedures Policy for Young People (contained in *Policy and Procedures for the Welfare of Young People in Rugby*).

Bullying

It is of paramount importance that all rugby clubs have in place an anti-bullying policy to which all players, coaches and parents subscribe. Bullying is not always easy to define or identify and will not always be an adult abusing a young person; it is often the case that the bully is a young person. There are three main types of bullying:

Physical

For example, hitting, kicking or theft. Physical abuse among children can sometimes be hard to notice because it's often done slyly, when the coach or teacher isn't looking. Encourage victims or onlookers to let you know when it's happening. Do not allow a 'bystander' culture where children see bullying but do nothing about it. Remember that theft can also include extortion, such as 'Give us a pound (or drink, sweets and so on) and I'll leave you alone.'

Verbal

For example, racist or homophobic remarks such as 'Stupid black kid', 'Nutty Moslem' or 'you're gay'.

Emotional

For example, persistent negative feedback such as 'Useless idiot', 'You couldn't catch a ball properly if you had Velcro gloves on' or 'You lot were useless today, utter rubbish.'

All of these will include:

■ deliberate hostility and aggression towards a victim or group

■ a victim who is weaker and less powerful than the bully or bullies

■ an outcome that is always painful and distressing for the individuals.

Bullying behaviour may also include:

■ other forms of violence, such as intimidation, barging or tripping up. This may not necessarily occur on the field of play; very often it's in the changing rooms;

■ sarcasm, spreading rumours and persistent teasing. Sarcasm and spreading rumours are never acceptable, but sometimes teasing forms part of a healthy friendship, such as light banter, a joke and a laugh between friends. However, when it becomes persistent, nasty and hurtful it must be stopped;

■ tormenting, ridiculing or humiliation. There is no excuse for this behaviour by adults in charge of children, but among the children themselves this form of bullying often goes on in changing rooms or other areas where the children congregate without the adults being around. Be vigilant. Do spot checks and encourage players to come to you in confidence if this is occurring;

■ graffiti or gestures. Graffiti of any kind, anywhere, is antisocial and vandalises property. It may include writing on another player's sports kit or bag. It's not cool and it should not be tolerated. Gestures too can say as much as words and must be stopped if they are used to intimidate, criticise or humiliate anyone, whether child or adult;

■ unwanted physical contact or abusive, offensive comments of a sexual nature.

The competitive nature of rugby union makes it a potential environment for the bully. Snuff it out in your club or school.

What to look for outside your club or school

Be aware of potential abuse outside your tag rugby club or school, but note that such indicators as untreated injuries, seemingly over-enthusiastic coaches, children who appear withdrawn and so on are not necessarily proof that the young person is being abused. Sometimes changes in behaviour can relate to other significant events in a young person's life, such as bereavement, internal family difficulties or bullying. Working in partnership with parents and carers and ensuring positive communication between everyone will help to ensure that reasons for changes in behaviour can be identified and action taken to support the young person.

What to do if you have suspicions about any kind of abuse within the club or school

This includes anything listed above. If you have suspicions, follow the procedures as laid out in the RFU, RFUW and the NSPCC's *Policy and Procedures for the Welfare of Young People in Rugby Union*.

It is *not* the responsibility of those working in rugby union to decide that abuse is occurring, but it *is* their responsibility to act on any concern. Non-action is not an option. The welfare of the young person or persons is paramount. Once the RFU Ethics and Equity Manager is informed, the RFU will take action and you can step back, having done your duty.

Health and Safety

Remember to implement the following:

- **no contact**: ensure that the players understand the difference between the very physical nature of senior rugby and the non-contact element of tag rugby, and explain why;
- **safe environment**: ensure that players are safe from physical, emotional and sexual harm;
- **first aid**: having a basic knowledge of first aid will help to deal with the injury and assess whether it is minor or serious.

Also be aware of the following:

- disability: be aware of simple measures for coping with disabilities such as epilepsy or diabetes;
- children in wheelchairs: this has been dealt with in detail in Chapters 3–6;
- children with learning difficulties: be aware of the need for extra care for children who may have Down's syndrome and other such disabilities, but don't be fearful of these children playing tag rugby;

■ a real emergency: serious injury in tag rugby is rare, but if it happens don't panic. Know what to do and when to summon an ambulance.

But remember...

Don't think that this all sounds too much like doom and gloom. The vast majority of children are well looked after by their parents or carers and you may never encounter any of the problems detailed above. Remember to be on your guard, know what to look for and how to act on it and then go and enjoy your rugby along with all the players.

The Tigers – Winners of the Salisbury Under-7s Festival 2005–6: (l-r) William Gatehouse, Thomas Roberts, Tom Kuhle, Philip Allison (holding trophy), Jon Burton (head coach), Henry Emmett, Callum McTaggart, Archie Bourne, Sam Chester.

9 | **funding and festivals**

Starting a club is one thing; funding it and keeping it going is another. You will need basic equipment such as size 3 rugby balls, tag belts and markers, you may have to pay rent on a ground or clubhouse and you may also have other expenses such as electricity and heating. One of the most effective ways of funding is to have a subscription charge for all players, payable at the beginning of each season. Minis at Salisbury pay £30 each, which also covers insurance for the players. If you join in with an established club you will, of course, cut your costs by being able to share the expenses.

Alternatively, you could run your own fundraising events. There are many festivals and competitions already in place for tag rugby players, clubs and schools, but there's nothing to stop you from running one of your own. However, in order to do this it is essential that you prepare thoroughly before any other teams enter your grounds. There is also a wide variety of national and local funding agencies that can provide support for your school or club's project or needs (see pages 114–5).

Fundraising events

Festivals, competitions and fundraising events are fundamental to the lifeblood of a club or school. You could run your own Tag Rugby Festival or Cup Competition, or have an event such as a barbecue, quiz night, bring and buy sale or Christmas party. Most important of all, events like this are great fun and bring people together for a common purpose. Social networks are established, friendships are made and clubs and school teams are strengthened.

How do we stage one?

The most efficient and successful way to run or take part in events is to set up an events committee. Schools can call on parents' associations as well as the school's own resources, and clubs will have social committees and members who are willing and able to help out. This leaves playing and training to the teachers and coaches, who have enough to do without operational aspects and fundraising.

Setting up a committee

Any event, whether it's a barbecue or an area Tag Rugby Festival, needs to be planned well in advance and will require lots of people with different talents and expertise. This means that the workload and responsibilities can be shared and will not depend on one driven person. Make sure that each member of the committee knows what his or her role is. This will maximise efficiency and ensure that the same task isn't duplicated by people who have no idea what other people are doing. Don't fall into the trap of having too many chiefs. Have one person in overall charge and make this clear to other members of the committee. Full co-operation is essential. The Event Director does not have to be the chair of the committee, nor does it have to be the same person each time. Choose the person who has the most experience and interest in that particular event. The events committee could also co-opt members of other committees in your club or school, such as the social committee, who can take care of catering, publicity and so on. The following is a recommended committee structure, but is not written in stone. You may want to adapt it to your particular circumstances.

- **Event Director**: oversees the whole event.
- **Festival/Competition Manager**: organises all aspects of the structure of the event.
- **Promotions Manager**: responsible for publicity and sponsorship.
- **Site Manager**: responsible for all equipment and facilities needed on the day.
- **Volunteer Manager**: recruits potential volunteers and co-ordinates their duties.
- **Treasurer**: someone trustworthy and knowledgeable about accounting.

The Event Director:

- oversees the whole event
- is the person most qualified to run this particular event
- determines how the event is to be run
- makes the final decisions on event developments.

The Festival/Competition Manager:

- sends out entry forms and covering letters to schools, clubs, companies and colleges
- organises the structure of the event, who will play who, times, pitch and referee
- organises referees, scorekeepers and other personnel needed for the day

- gets the event covered by insurance
- sends out event programmes and relevant information to participants.

The Promotions Manager:
- seeks sponsors, such as Sportsmatch and Awards for All funding (see pages 114–5 for more information)
- produces the programme
- informs the media
- produces certificates
- organises trophies and medals
- designs a T-shirt for volunteers and referees, if funds allow.

The Site Manager:
- makes sure all equipment needed is provided, including size 3 rugby balls, tags and tag belts
- ensures all facilities are in place
- produces score desks
- oversees marking of the pitches
- organises a first-aid station and officer
- organises refreshments
- organises a public address system and/or two-way radios
- is responsible for display boards
- oversees entertainment.

The Volunteer Manager:
- provides a focal point for volunteers
- attends events, festivals and socials to encourage and stimulate interest in new volunteers
- recruits potential volunteers
- welcomes new volunteers and keeps them informed of relevant information
- co-ordinates the volunteer workforce throughout the event.

What type of event should we have?

You need to do the following:

- Decide which type of event suits your club/school best, where it will take place and who will take part in it.

- Decide what is to be achieved from the event.

- Make sure you can fund it. Look at the suggestions for grants and awards on pages 114–5, which may cover some of your costs.

- Choose a date and time that doesn't clash with something similar in your area.

- Make sure that you have enough personnel/volunteers free to cover the entire event.

- Involve parents/carers and other members of your school or club.

Points to remember before you start

- **Treasurer**: you must set a budget and stick to it.

- **Promotions Manager**: it's your job to generate as much publicity as possible so that you get the required number of players and people involved to make this a fantastic success.

- **Co-ordinators**: you must ensure that the venue is suitable and has disabled access.

Free stuff!

The Promotions Manager should try to get as much for free as he or she can by approaching potential sponsors for catering, prizes and publicity. What can you offer potential sponsors in return for their financial support or free goods? If you can offer something worthwhile, they will support the event. Examples of what you could offer include:

- advertising space at the club, particularly on match days

- the chance to display merchandise: a car dealer could bring along one of the latest models to park and display at the club, which could lead to test drives or orders

- publicity in the local newspaper, any relevant magazines and other similar publications

- official acknowledgement as a supporter of the club

- free or discount tickets for match events (especially at clubs like Harlequins)

- the chance for others to see you're a good citizen!

How to get started

- Send out covering letters with details of the event and application forms to your target schools, clubs or organisations.

- Have a small flyer/poster to include with the covering letters, which will make the event very attractive to your targets.

- Decide on the fee level for entry into the competition or event.

- Book referees and organise scorekeepers and other personnel needed for the day.

- Make sure the event is covered by insurance.

- Have a great time!

Funding

There is a wide variety of national and local funding agencies that can provide support for your club's project. In general, this funding support will either be in the form of revenue (people and projects) or capital (facilities and equipment).

How can I find funding?

Contact your RFU Rugby Development Officer (RDO) for advice, and look at the information below on organisations that provide funding. You will also need to work out your 'Three Os':

1. **Objective** – what do you aim to achieve?
2. **Output** – how will you deliver it?
3. **Outcome** – what difference will your project make?

Most importantly, do your homework! Thoroughly research the funding organisations and make sure the one you choose is the right one for your project. This is extremely important because you may have a very good case for a grant, but if you approach the wrong organisation it will not consider your application and it will all have been a hugely disappointing waste of time, skills and money. So, choose the funding organisation wisely, prepare your case really well and go for it!

Engaging a professional fundraiser

It's possible that your case will be better presented and have a greater chance of success if you use a professional fundraiser, but this will cost you so make sure that you have a good chance of being successful.

Sources of funding

Here are some sources of application for funding. It is not an exhaustive list and sometimes a particular source may cease to operate for one reason or another. Also look at what other clubs have achieved in the Community Rugby section on the RFU website, or use a search engine to find a club in your area.

Awards for All

Awards for All is a Lottery grants scheme aimed at local communities. It awards grants to voluntary sports organisations such as rugby clubs, schools or colleges linking with local clubs, voluntary groups, disability groups, women's organisations, ethnic community groups and neighbourhood associations playing or planning to play sport. You can apply all year round and there are no deadlines. For further information, visit www.awardsforall.org.uk or email awardsforallinfo@rfu.com.

Talent Ladder

Visit the website www.talentladder.org.uk for up-to-date information for teachers, coaches, players and parents, including competition information.

The Big Lottery Fund

The Big Lottery Fund funds charities and the voluntary sector within sport. The fund focuses on smaller grants at local level and big capital projects, intended to regenerate and revitalise communities. For further information, visit www.biglotteryfund.org.uk.

The Coalfields Regeneration Trust

The Coalfields Regeneration Trust is an independent grant-making body registered with the Charity Commission and dedicated to the regeneration of the coalfield communities. For further information, visit www.coalfields-regen.org.uk.

The Foundation for Sport and the Arts

The Foundation for Sport and the Arts is an independent discretionary trust funded by the Football Pools. It has provided significant capital funding for rugby union and other sports in recent years. For further information, visit www.thefsa.net.

Grants website

Voluntary and community organisations have access to £182 million of government funding. For further information, visit www.governmentfunding.org.uk.

Local authorities

The amount of funding available and the organisations that qualify will vary from one authority to another. Most have their own websites and phone numbers can be found in local directories.

National Association of Councils for Voluntary Service

For further information, visit www.nacvs.org.uk.

The Rugby Football Foundation

The Rugby Football Foundation invests in community rugby facilities via the Community Rugby Capital Fund. The overall aim of the scheme is to finance capital projects to improve facilities and contribute to the recruitment and retention of community rugby players. All clubs at levels 5 and below in the English Clubs Rugby Union Championship (i.e. the leagues) are eligible to apply to the fund. For further information, visit www.rfu.com/microsites/rff.

Sport England and UK Sport – Community Investment Fund

Rugby Union is one of the most important sports to which Sport England and UK Sport will give priority for funding. Both these organisations are sponsored by the government. Decisions about Sport England funding (grants over £5000) are made locally by the nine regional sports boards. For further information, visit www.sportengland.org or www.uksport.gov.uk.

Sportsmatch

Sportsmatch is funded by the Department for Culture, Media and Sport to support the development of grass-roots sport in England. They have approximately £3 million per year to award. For further information, visit www.sportsmatch.co.uk.

Fundraising support

The following web-based agencies can provide software and support to your club, and can help locate suitable funding agencies in your local area:

www.access-funds.co.uk – grant information for UK voluntary and non-profit organisations
www.acf.org.uk – Association of Charitable Foundations
www.ccpr.org.uk – Central Council for Physical Recreation
www.charitychoice.co.uk – an encyclopedia of charities on the internet
www.funderfinder.org.uk – software to help you find funds
www.fundinginformation.org – up-to-date information on funding sources
www.grantsnet.co.uk – UK grants and funding information
www.sponsorship-advice.org – Sports Sponsorship Advisory Service
www.sportslink.info – online funding listings
www.sports-sponsorship.co.uk – Institute of Sports Sponsorship

appendix 1:
The RFU's Fair Play Codes

These Codes are very helpful for the smooth running of a club or matches. There are Codes for coaches, players, parents/carers, spectators and match officials. They can be photocopied and given out to the appropriate groups.

The RFU Good Coach's Code

In rugby union, coaches of young players should:

- Recognise the importance of fun and enjoyment.
- Realise that most learning is achieved through doing.
- Appreciate that the needs of the players come before the needs of the sport.
- Be a positive role model.
- Foster a good sports attitude and keep winning and losing in perspective.
- Respect all refereeing decisions and ensure that your players do the same.
- Discuss your team's performance with them in a positive way, which will encourage them; criticism will crush their spirit.
- Adjust coaching to the level of the young players' experience, physique, physical abilities and mental development.
- Ensure a safe environment, with adequate first aid.
- Use a squad system to avoid overuse of the best players and to ensure that all players get a chance to play.
- Never allow a player to train or play when injured.
- Ensure good supervision of young players, both on and off the field.
- Ensure that young players do not train or play in extremes of heat or cold, or where there is unacceptable risk of injury.
- Develop an awareness of nutrition and communicate this to young players as part of their lifestyle management.
- Ensure that their coaching keeps up to date with RFU codes and rules.
- Know and adhere to the policies and procedures outlined in Chapter 8 and in the RFU Child Protection Guidance Booklet.

The RFU Good Parent's and Carer's Code

Parents/carers are encouraged to:

■ Be familiar with the coaching and training programme and keep it in the diary.

■ Ensure your child is fully involved in the club or team.

■ Let coaches know if your child can't get to a session.

■ Become involved and offer assistance or expertise.

■ Help coaches all you can with supervising the players.

■ Offer transport to away games.

■ If you have any concerns, let the coaches know.

■ Support the Good Coach's Code.

Parents/carers should also know that:

■ Coaches should recognise the importance of fun and enjoyment for young players.

■ Winning and losing is part of the game and players should be encouraged to accept both with dignity and praise for all players.

Parents/carers should:

■ Show appreciation that all coaches, helpers, referees and other officials give up their precious free time for your child's enjoyment.

■ Remember that rugby is primarily for the child's enjoyment, not just yours.

■ Always encourage a child to play, but never force them.

■ Focus on effort rather than winning or losing.

■ Be aware of a child's capabilities and don't push them towards a level they won't be able to achieve.

■ Provide positive comments in training and during the game.

■ Be aware that negative comments undermine everyone's confidence and are unpleasant.

■ Support the club or school in not tolerating loud or abusive behaviour from anyone, players or spectators.

■ Respect decisions made by the match officials and encourage all children to do the same.

■ Be a good role model.

The RFU Good Player's Code

Players are encouraged to:

- Appreciate the efforts made by coaches, assistants, match officials and administrators in providing the opportunity for you to play tag rugby.

- Have loyalty and commitment to the adults and your team-mates.

- Know that you have the right to be in a safe environment free from all types of abuse from adults and fellow team players.

- Know that you have the right to tell an adult, who belongs to the club or school or is outside of it, if you feel that you are not being treated properly by an adult or fellow team players.

Players should:

- Play because you want to, not because your coach or parents want you to.

- Realise that improving your skills and fun and enjoyment of the game are more important than winning or losing.

- Pay attention at training sessions.

- Work as hard for the team as you do for yourself.

- Be a good sport – win or lose.

- Play to the rules of tag rugby and accept, without any argument, all referees' decisions.

- Not allow your emotions to result in your physically or verbally abusing your team-mates, opponents or match officials.

- Treat everyone with respect in the way that you'd like to be treated yourself.

The RFU Good Spectator's Code

Spectators are encouraged to:

- Act as positive role models to all young players.

- Abide by the RFU Guidelines for Working with Children (see Chapter 8).

- Support the club or school in not tolerating loud or abusive behaviour from anyone, players or other spectators.

Spectators should:

- Remember that participation in sport is for the child's enjoyment.

- Accept that your enjoyment comes from theirs.

- Be sporting towards other teams.

- Respect match officials' decisions and remember that they are volunteers giving up their time so that your child can play tag rugby.

- Never verbally abuse anyone involved in the game as it undermines both officials and players and provides a negative role model for players to copy.

- Shout to encourage the players, not moan at them.

- Encourage all players regardless of their ability.

- Remember that ridicule is cruel and destructive.

The RFU Good Match Official's Code

Match Officials should:

- Recognise the importance of fun and enjoyment for young players.
- Comment in a constructive and encouraging way during games.
- Uphold the spirit of the game.
- Put the needs of young players before the needs of the sport.
- Understand the physical, social and emotional development of young children.
- Be a positive role model by setting a good example.
- Progress within the game by participating in courses such as Mini/Midi or National 15-a-side.

Match Officials must:

- Recognise that the safety of young players is paramount.
- Explain decisions as all young players are continuing to learn.
- Always penalise foul play.
- Play advantage whenever possible in order to let the game flow.
- Show that you understand the age and ability of young players.
- Be consistent and objective.
- Ensure that verbal abuse from players, coaches or spectators is not tolerated and is dealt with by club officials immediately.
- Be aware of and abide by the RFU Child Protection Guide (see Chapter 8).

index

index

Notes